"Stella Ellis is a strong, beautiful, desirable woman who shines inside and out. I am very excited about this book and believe women can learn a lot from Stella about being sexy and just feeling good about themselves."

—THIERRY MUGLER, FASHION DESIGNER

"I love Stella. She is my new muse."

—JEAN PAUL GAULTIER

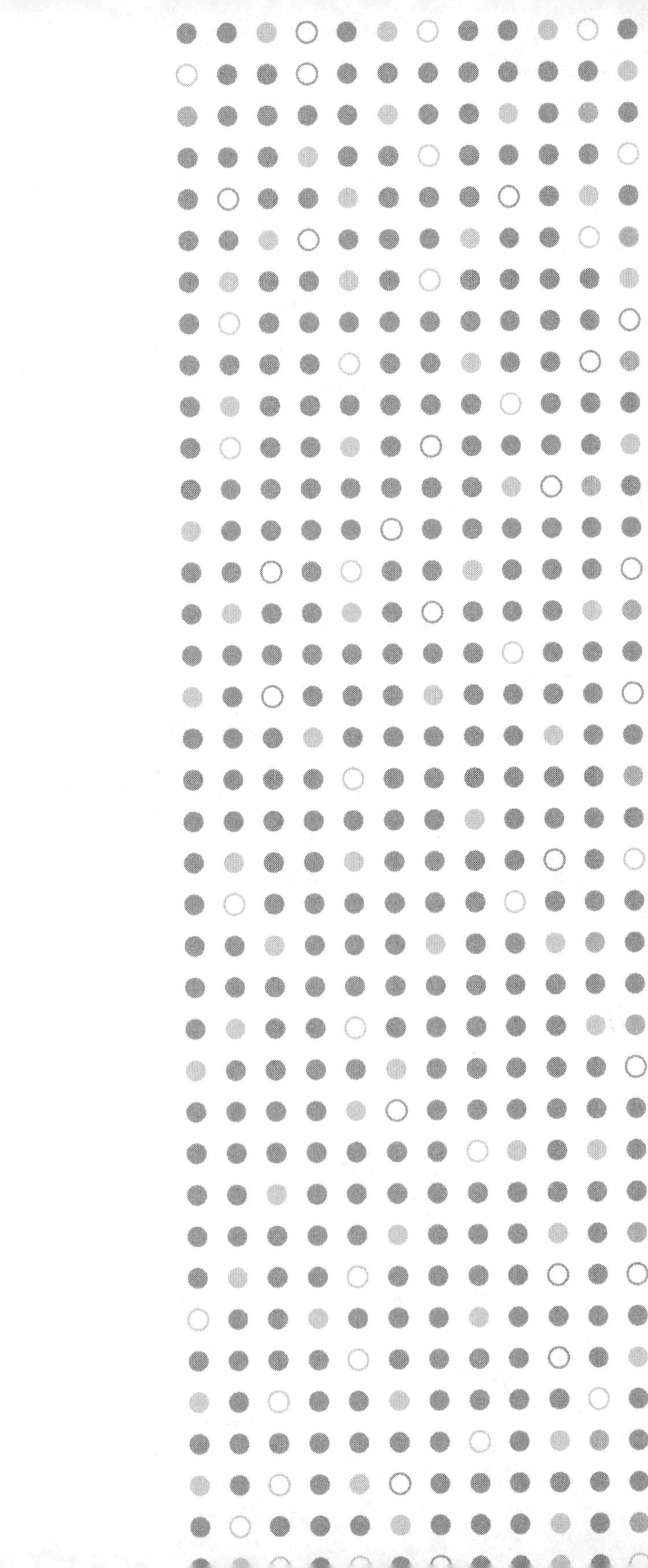

How to Look Good, Feel Good, and Be Happy—at *Any Size*

size**sexy**

stella ellis

Avon, Massachusetts

Published by
Adams Media, a division of F+W Media, Inc.
57 Littlefield Street, Avon, MA 02322. U.S.A.
www.adamsmedia.com

ISBN 10: 1-60550-355-X
ISBN 13: 978-1-60550-355-4
eISBN 10: 1-4405-0707-4
eISBN 13: 978-1-4405-0707-6

Printed in the United States of America.

10 9 8 7 6 5 4 3 2 1

Library of Congress Cataloging-in-Publication Data
is available from the publisher.

This book is dedicated to my husband and the special man in my life, Dov Berenzveig. Thank you for putting sexy in my size! For supporting me and encouraging me to follow my dreams. For always being there for me. For your patience, passion, and love. For making me feel beautiful and sexy all the time—no matter what. Size Sexy *would not be possible without it all. You're an amazing powerful and talented man. I love you with all my heart.*

contents

appendix

acknowledgments

I want to thank my parents, Marie and Simon Amar, for giving me love and affection. For making my childhood full of adventure and fun. For giving me endless opportunities and allowing me to follow my dreams. They taught me how to be self confident, worldly, and adventurous. From my mother, I got my sense of style, elegance, and ability to stay positive no matter what. From my father, I got my sense of wisdom and my hunger for knowledge, and I learned how to enjoy the good and luxurious pleasures of life. Both taught me all about the "*Joie de Vivre*."

To my siblings, David, Batya, and Joseph (Jojo), the great chef and a born comedian. I love them for giving me all the love in the world even though I have always lived far away from them. They have always supported all my ventures. To my sister-in-laws and my nieces and nephews—I love you all.

To my favorite cousin Jack Ohayon. Thank you for being there whenever I needed you while writing this book. Thank you for making time for me when I know you did not have it. You are a genius man and have countless amazing qualities. You are a true friend.

To my favorite aunt Lana for making my move to New York possible and for always being there for me.

To my uncle Jacob for always wanting to keep all the family close together and always being there when needed—you are a very kind and sweet man and I love you for that.

To my cousin Alix Malka for being there at the right place at the right time and for your exceptional generosity. I will always cherish the fabulous times and all the fun we had together.

To Jean Paul Gaultier and Thierry Mugler—thank you for giving me your runways and for letting me swing my big hips and flaunt my assets on them. You are both geniuses in more ways than one!

Thank you to all my friends for all your love and support—you all know who you are.

To my agent, Lynne Rabinoff, for making this book a reality. Thank you for being a strong woman who always looks out for my best interests. You are one tough cookie and my kind of girl!

Thank you to Kim Potts, my editors Chelsea King and Katie Corcoran Lytle, and to everyone at Adams Media for getting this book off the ground and into the hands of all the fabulous *Size Sexy* women around the world.

introduction

breaking

My inspiration for doing this book came when I was working as a model for French fashion designers Jean Paul Gaultier and Thierry Mugler (more on that in Chapter 1). Doing those runway shows and walking out in front of the fabulous fashion crowds wearing amazing, custom-created couture allowed me to show who I am—my gregarious personality, my self-confidence, my generous curves, the way I carry myself, the way I dress. Even before Gaultier's shows, I was very confident, very outgoing, very comfortable, very sexy, and very fabulous, but during those shows I was exposed to a larger audience. I got great feedback from people, both from the crowd and from admirers. I would meet up with women who were also on the curvaceous side; they would come up to me and tell me how great I looked and how much they admired my self-confidence, when they were struggling so much in their own lives, with their weight, their figures.

I knew then that it was time for all these women to stop worrying, to start letting go of this constant obsession with their size, and to find a size that was comfortable and healthy for them. I thought they could learn a few things from me in that area, learn how to find confidence and self-acceptance within themselves and bring their inner stylistas out for the rest of the world to see. This is especially important for young women who think they can't be happy because they're not a size 0 or 2 or 4 or 6 or 10.

the mold

When I met those women who came up to me after fashion shows, I listened to them and understood exactly where they were coming from. They are what really made me want to write this book, to share my secrets, my experiences, and my attitude about my body, my size, and my weight. I want to tell these women who struggle with their weight that they are not alone; *Size Sexy* women are everywhere!

I also want to show them that they can be self-accepting, happy, and stylish in their lives, just as I have been in my life on the fashion runways and in my everyday life. This book is about teaching you to believe in your beauty, to stop letting your weight and your feelings about your weight rule your life. That's what I did. I chose a certain path, which I'll share with you throughout this book. That decision and my commitment to living my life that way has taken me to some amazing and wonderful places, and it can do the same for you, in your own world, with your own dreams.

Beauty is everywhere, if you only have the eyes to see it. Hopefully, while you are reading *Size Sexy*, you will come to see the beauty in being a *Size Sexy* woman, and more importantly, will come to see the beauty in yourself.

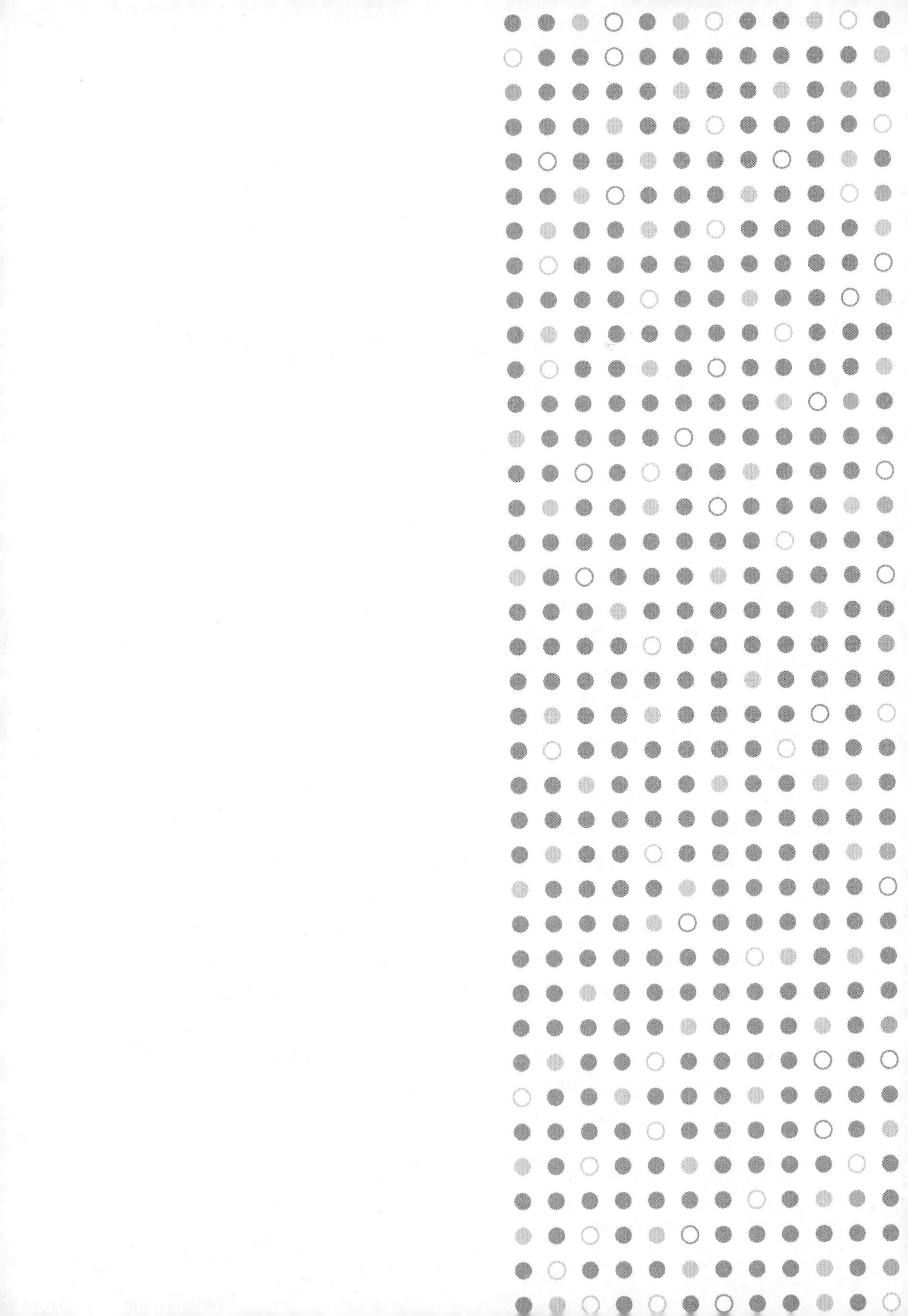

chapter **one**

introducing . . . stella!

In 1992, the fabulous French fashion designer Jean Paul Gaultier, whose muse I would become, invited me to participate in a runway show in Los Angeles for the wonderful AIDS charity amfAR. The event was star-studded—it's still famous for a wonderfully over-the-top moment in which Madonna stole the show by walking down the runway topless, save for a pair of suspenders—and Gaultier invited *me* to participate.

It would be one of the biggest and most glamorous shows of my fashion career and I was thrilled, not only because it was such an important cause, but also because it was going to be an amazing, once-in-a-lifetime occasion. It would take place at the Shrine Auditorium in LA (where the Oscars were held), so you can imagine the kind of grand atmosphere we expected and created. With the setting and the 6,000 people attending, the show felt like a rock concert for supermodels. It was very exciting to be on such a big stage and to mingle with the amazing talents who were involved with the gala—Billy Idol, Anthony Kiedis, Lorraine Bracco, Luther Vandross, Faye Dunaway, Raquel Welch, Patti LaBelle, and many others. I had modeled in shows with supermodels at this point, but this amfAR show, with all these fabulous and creative people taking part and gathered in one place, promised to be something far beyond my experiences and my expectations.

I didn't know how I was going to be received in America. Paris, where I had walked in Gaultier's runway shows, was a much smaller venue. This event felt intimidating because it was so large—not another runway show with a few rows of people on each side. I was confident in my abilities, but I still didn't know how this predominantly American crowd would react to me. Fortunately, I worried for no reason. Madonna's bold fashion statement stole the show, but when I came out people began clapping, cheering, and calling out my name! It was an incredible, incredible high, and a feeling of being big and beautiful. At the end of the show, everyone who had participated came out onto the stage, holding hands while receiving a standing ovation—it was amazing. Although it was the peak of my collaborations with Gaultier, it was just another fabulous moment in a career that had afforded me the opportunity to show the fashion industry—and the world—that we full-figured girls can strut our stuff with the best of them, literally, with the best, most fabulous, gorgeous, celebrated actors, actresses, singers, and supermodels in the world. The *Size Sexy* revolution was in full swing!

fabulous quotes

"I've never known what it is I was supposed to have had. All I do know is that sex appeal isn't make-believe. It's not the way you look or the way you walk or the way you smile, it's the way you are."
—Lana Turner, Hollywood Icon

High on Fashion

So how did a full-figured woman like me end up in one of Gaultier's fashion shows? Well, in 1990, I had just gone through a painful divorce after a five-year marriage in Los Angeles when I decided to move to New York City and break into the fashion world as a makeup artist. I was a voluptuous girl going out into the single world, but I wasn't intimidated by my new status. I didn't think that, because I was no longer in a relationship, I had to lose weight or make any dramatic physical changes to go where I wanted to be going. I started working as a makeup artist, and my cousin and friend Alix Malka, who had worked with designer Thierry Mugler for many years, introduced me to Mugler in New York. He and I clicked. He was doing grand, glamorous, creative shows, and I was thrilled when I was asked to do the makeup for some of the shows. I became a part of Stéphane Marais's group of makeup artists, and we worked throughout Fashion Week in Paris, on shows for designers from John Galliano to Chanel.

I was a big girl—curvaceous and outgoing—and I had no problem socializing with people or with having people be attracted to me and wanting to spend time with me. People had a perception of me as being this fabulous, gorgeous, interesting person to be around, and I didn't have a problem with that—or with my size or with expressing myself through the way I dressed. Quite the contrary, I wore my hair big and perfectly coifed. My makeup was always done flawlessly, and I dressed in fabulous bustiers that showed off my décolletage, small waist, and big hips. In fact, bustiers and corsets were a big part of my signature style, and I owned them in many colors and fabrics, including several vintage bustiers from the '50s and '60s that I had bought in Hollywood, New York, and Paris. I enhanced my signature style with jet-black hair, long red fingernails, and red-hot lipstick.

My Big Break

One day in 1992, I was invited, with Alix, to a Vivienne Westwood fashion show in Paris. We were sitting in the front row—me dressed to the hilt in one of my marvelous bustiers—and opposite us, across the runway, sat Jean Paul Gaultier, a very talented, creative, famous fashion designer. He was sitting with Myriam Schaefer, a woman who had worked with him for many years. She was a friend of Alix's who I had met on a few occasions, so we all waved to each other across the runway.

Throughout the show, every time I glanced his way, Gaultier was looking back at me. I found out later he had been asking Myriam all kinds of questions about who I was and telling her how amazing I looked. She told him that I was a makeup artist from New York and later, backstage at the post-runway show cocktail party, Myriam introduced us. As soon as the designer and I launched into a conversation, he admitted that he was fascinated with my look. He told me that I had an amazing shape, that I was very sexy and feminine, and that he had decided we should have dinner and get to know each other. We continued to chitchat and laugh and then made arrangements to meet for dinner. I was very excited, of course, to have an opportunity to know such an interesting man. A couple of days later we *did* meet for dinner and during the main course Gaultier said something that pleasantly surprised me. "You are really so fabulous," he said, "I would like to have you in one of my shows."

I thought it was genius, but it honestly took a minute for me to digest what he was really saying. I immediately received his offer as a wonderful acknowledgment of my style and personality and the kind of strong, fierce person I have always been, but, as you can imagine, that kind of offer by someone of Gaultier's creativity and caliber left me reeling with incredible feelings. Of course I quickly said, "Yes, with pleasure."

*fabulous*quotes

"Any woman can look her best if she feels good in her skin. It's not a question of clothes and makeup. It's how she sparkles."
—Sophia Loren

Afterwards, I did worry somewhat about what he had in mind. He had told me that he thought I was fabulous and beautiful and sexy and that was what had captured his attention, but what were his intentions for me in his show? How did he see me on the runway? Would he present me the way I was, or did he have something else in mind? Did he want to portray me like someone out of a Fellini film: dark, fanciful, provocative? There was nothing wrong with that if that was what he had in mind—I had always felt like a marvelous, seductive Fellini-esque creature. The talented Italian director had a flair for showing unique people and different personalities in his films.

Larger Than Life by Gaultier

I asked Gaultier what he had in mind, and he said he wanted to bring out exactly how I looked, but to make it even bigger, to make it larger than life. As I mentioned, at that time, I was wearing a lot of bustiers, very tight clothes that showed off my curves and my small waist, with high heels, big boobs, long nails, high hairdos, red lips. I was very feminine, very sexy, very outgoing, and that's exactly what Jean Paul was telling me he wanted to capture for an even bigger crowd on the runway. He wanted to represent me through his eyes, through his designs, clothing designs that he wanted to create for my "generous shape," as he phrased it.

The minute he said that, I thought, "Perfect, beautiful, I'm being acknowledged for the way I look. I'm being acknowledged for my size, my shape, my sexiness." Even though he was always attracted to the individual, to the personalities of the models, Gaultier was someone who dressed skinny girls all the time. To me, this invitation was a huge "Hallelujah to the big girls!" It was absolute acceptance on the biggest runway in the fashion world—a big girl was going to walk that sacred fashion runway, something that had never been done before!

Gaultier arranged for me to visit his atelier, his studio, to discuss the show and, when I saw the outfit he had in mind for me, I could not have been more excited. He was creating a corset dress with strings pulled from top to bottom—drawing my boobs together to create an impressive, flattering cleavage and cinching in my waist to accentuate my curvy hips. He also wanted to incorporate my trademark big hairdo. It felt so good to know that he really did want to play up the style I had created for myself, with his own interpretation, especially since he was already known for his fearless corsets and bustiers.

When it came time for the show in 1992, there was a lot of excitement, and, I'll admit, even a little bit of fear on my part. But I had loved, loved, loved the experience of going through fittings, discussing hair and makeup with Gaultier, watching him design the dress, and seeing him and his whole staff so excited about it. As the big day grew closer, I started to feel even more confident and fabulous.

Finally, the day of the show arrived, and I was indescribably excited. Being backstage was an amazing feeling; I was there with some of the most recognizable faces in the world, the supermodels of the fashion industry. Naomi Campbell, Linda Evangelista, Kate Moss, Christy Turlington, and Yasmeen Ghauri were among the models walking the runway that day—and I was sharing a dressing area with them.

It was thrilling for me to arrive backstage as a big girl, feeling so curvaceous and voluptuous even when surrounded by all these famous skinny models. With all my size and sexiness, I felt glamorous, and I experienced an overwhelming sense of achievement; Gaultier had sought me out. My look had captured his attention, and now he was going to show me off, celebrate *me*, in front of one of the most discriminating crowds in all of the fashion industry.

Being selected by Gaultier truly confirmed for me that no matter what size you are, no matter how big you are, your life is all about what you reflect, what you project to people, on the outside. Success is all about self-acceptance, having a vivacious personality and the femininity that comes from that, which will help people see you the way you want to be seen, no matter your size, shape, or age. Who you are comes from the inside.

Showtime!

The next step in getting ready for Gaultier's show was getting dressed and going onstage. I was giving myself a pep talk the whole time: "Okay, Stella, you have to walk that runway, girl! Flaunt your assets, own that runway, be positive, and, even if no one is clapping or cheering, you have to keep your head up and do your thing!" And, of course, I got a lot of support and kisses and hugs from Gaultier. "Go show them yourself," he said simply.

And for a moment, when I first edged onto that runway, I experienced something akin to a little blackout. For the first few seconds—which felt like eternity—I really didn't know what to expect. Then, at the moment that I fully stepped onto the stage and into the spotlight, the audience at that show—fashion editors, journalists, TV media, photographers, actors, and celebrities—screamed and shouted and clapped like crazy!

Since I had primed myself by saying, "Girl, you have to keep going, no matter what," I walked like I was the only woman on the runway, like I belonged there and no one could have told me differently. And people were going crazy, clapping with admiration. When I reached the end of the runway, the photographers were all snapping away and screaming, "Stella! Stella! Stand still; don't move!"

It was a revolution! A revolution of sizes, a revolution of perception, and a revolution of beauty that happened at that moment, as the photographers' flashes continued going off all around me and the crowd continued to erupt in applause. I executed my u-turn and walked toward backstage and, by the time I got there, I was shaking with excitement, so thrilled that the show had turned out like this. Gaultier and I jumped on each other and hugged and kissed, and he said to me, "I told you, I told you they were going to go crazy for you! I told you that you were going to be fabulous!"

fabulous quotes

"If a girl has curviness, exciting lips, and a certain breathlessness, it helps. And it won't do a bit of harm if she also has a kittenish, soft and cuddly quality."
—Jayne Mansfield, Bombshell Actress

Of course, I had had my doubts in the beginning, but Gaultier, who had that eye, that visual talent, that intuition for spotting and celebrating people who are strong in their personalities and possess unique looks, had forged an incredible collaboration between us.

That was my very first runway show and from there it was like magic. There were pictures everywhere in the media the next day. There had been a celebratory cocktail party after the show and, in the days that followed, there were more parties, more dinners with people, more attention from those in the fashion world.

Strolling Down the Runway with the Boys

Gaultier also asked me to participate in his men's shows, which made me feel quite special, because female models weren't usually invited to participate. During one such show, Boy George was the star attraction. Backstage, the singer and I really clicked, and when one of his musicians began playing the guitar backstage, Boy George started singing and I joined in. He was really surprised that I actually had a nice voice, and we had a fun, fabulous, spontaneous moment together—a moment I had created while surrounded by all those gorgeous, naked men, all of whom loved and adored walking the runway with me. It felt very seductive to be a part of that.

Later, Gaultier called and he told me that he wanted me to participate in the ad campaign for the collection he had just shown on the runway. That was even more confirmation that I had been admired by the fashion crowd. Not that that was the most important thing, however; what mattered most was that I had accepted the first challenge and was happy with myself for doing so. But now Gaultier was asking me to participate in his campaign, which meant photo shoots and appearing in all the biggest fashion magazines all over the world, like *French Vogue*, *ELLE*, *Italian Vogue*, etc. It also meant more exposure, more work, more admiration for who I am. Of course, I said "yes" right away.

The photos, which were going to be shot by Gaultier personally, brought about another new opportunity, and another chance for my personality and style to shine. The runway show was one thing, but photos were another. Would I prove to be photogenic? What about the particulars of fashion photography, the angles, being able to emote so the photographer can capture it on film? It was a whole new world, but, by following Jean Paul's direction and my intuition for posing, everything came out beautifully. The big hair, the big boobs—simply gorgeous! I felt big and glamorous standing there posing for the shots, and when we all looked at the Polaroids of the shoot everyone was wowed by how they had turned out. Experiencing this type of collaboration with such talented professionals and realizing how photogenic I was was an amazing feeling.

After the shoot for the ad campaign, I continued working as a makeup artist for other shows and then flew back home to New York while I waited for the Gaultier ads to debut in magazines. When they did—wow! There I was in *ELLE, Vanity Fair,. Glamour, French Vogue*, and *Italian Vogue*—the most influential fashion magazines of the day.

Gaultier also surprised me with a special limited edition Stella T-shirt. He had taken a photo where I looked like an opera diva and put in on a T-shirt that went on to become a bestseller. More than a year later, I was walking down the street in New York City and I saw my face looking back at me—a man was wearing one of the Gaultier Stella T-shirts.

And Then, Meisel Called

Around this time, Steven Meisel, one of the most respected and talented fashion photographers in the world, called Gaultier's office looking to get in touch with me. He wanted to arrange a photo shoot with me and some of the other models from the Gaultier show for a spread in *Italian Vogue*. This was another grand moment. Steven Meisel, a renowned photographer who shot layouts for the top fashion magazines and only worked with the top supermodels of the era, wanted to photograph me! I admired him tremendously for his work, his taste, his ideas. So of course I felt fabulous—how else could I feel? Here I was, a size 20, two times—actually, two and a half times!—the size of the other models (or, as I like to say, I have an hourglass-and-a-half-figure), and I was being admired by and invited to work with these visionaries who I had admired for so long.

My Triumphant Return

When I arrived in Paris for the Meisel shoot, I had no idea who the other models would be. When I arrived on the set, Steven Meisel was there to hug and greet me, and only then did I see the rest of the lineup: Linda, Christy, Naomi, Kate, Nadja Auermann, and Tanel, Gaultier's favorite male muse—in other words, the top supermodels of the day. All together, there were ten supermodels—and one big, voluptuous model—and yet I was very much one of the girls that day. They were professionals, but I was still new at this and I was very much looking forward to that exciting day. Meisel and I clicked right away; we had a great connection. He made me feel so comfortable and beautiful that the shoot went fabulously. I not only felt like I belonged, but I was so ecstatic about another amazing collaboration with another fashion icon that I left wondering, *Where is this going next?*

When the Meisel spread appeared in *Italian Vogue*, I was thrilled to be in a magazine where only skinny girls had appeared. And I was even more thrilled to discover, when opening the first double spread, that a photo of me—with my name—sat opposite the words "People in Paris" and consumed one whole page. *Un-be-lievable.* Being selected as the model whose photograph opens a fashion magazine spread meant that everyone from the photographer to the magazine editors had decided that I should appear first—before Linda Evangelista or Christy Turlington or Naomi Campbell or Nadja Auermann or Kate Moss. My sensational curves and self-confidence had paid off. And that was just the beginning. . . . New opportunities continued to come my way.

The next season, Gaultier asked me to work with him again, and it was another fabulous collection, with outfits for me that continued to show off my décolletage. Again, I received warm, enthusiastic receptions from the runway show crowds. I became more and more well known throughout the fashion industry, and it all felt wonderful. I was becoming this well-known fashion creature. I went back to Paris to let it all continue to unfold, appreciating myself and all that being myself was bringing into my life.

Becoming a Gaultier Muse

In 1993, Gaultier was fascinated with religious orthodox Jews and, after a great deal of research into their culture, decided to pull together a collection show using them as his inspiration. Being Jewish, I was very excited about this idea, particularly when he told me he was using me in that show as well. I was also beyond ecstatic, because, by that time, Gaultier had begun describing me as his muse in interviews. Thanks to Gaultier, everywhere I went people were approaching me to take pictures with them, the paparazzi were constantly snapping my picture, and I was being invited everywhere, to parties, to dinners. And things just continued to get better.

For this collection, Gaultier decided to make me a gorgeous corset dress and a huge, billowing cape with lots of fur around it and my name written in giant marabou letters on the back. During the show, he asked me to walk to the end of the runway, where the media photographers and the crowd were already going nuts, and to spread my arms out so that the name *Stella* would be spelled out loud and clear. Wow! I mean, wow! The audience's response was unbelievable! Where else could I want to go? How much more exposure and admiration was I going to get? It was amazing to be put up front so fabulously!

I adored walking the ramp and felt so gorgeous and proud and big and bodacious, wearing the long, beautiful cape with my name stitched so auspiciously on it. I was the queen of the event. I was large and in charge, and ruling the runway. Totally ruling the runway. People started to scream as soon as I appeared and when I walked to the front of the runway, spun around and spread my arms, the place erupted. The crowd jumped to its feet, people were yelling and taking photos, and the paparazzi were going mad. I turned around, threw everyone a big kiss, and then strutted back. The next day, pictures and articles appeared all over the press, chronicling the excitement and all the fabulousness. A few days later, Gaultier again called to say that he wanted me to be a part of the ad campaign for that collection.

Major excitement. We gathered for another photo shoot—the outfits, the hair, and the makeup were all top-notch. The photographer, Gaultier himself, snapped a group shot of a few of us models from that show, and then he used a close-up of my face to create a frame, which went all around the page, bordering the group shot. And I was huge—huge—at that time. I go through phrases of being big, bigger, and at times, a little smaller, and at that time I was at one of my biggest sizes. But when that layout appeared in all the fashion magazines, I was already recognizable in Paris, in New York, in London, and all throughout the fashion world, and I began to get calls from magazines that wanted to write articles and requests for interviews and for appearances in fashion shows all over the world.

The Mugler Moment

My friend Thierry Mugler also noticed that my modeling career had taken off. He told me how proud he was, and that he had been my friend from the beginning. "Everyone has used you in photo shoots and on the runway, and I was one of your first friends in the fashion world. One of the first people in the industry who admired the way you look and how you were so straightforward with your big mouth, with your attitude, and we've never done anything together," he told me. "I think it's about time that we do." We laughed about it, and then, of course, we started working together.

Now, mind you, Mugler was a whole different ballgame than Gaultier. The whole Mugler entourage and the people who come to see his shows were a very different crowd. Mugler liked women who were very skinny, very structured, and very small-waisted. He liked voluptuous, but in a different, thinner way than Gaultier. He created body-conscious clothing, so for Mugler to work with someone of my size was an extreme departure. But by that time, I was already known in the fashion world because of the media exposure and because a lot of people go from one show to another.

My first Mugler show occurred in 1994, and it was fabulous. Mugler liked to act more as a director of his shows, something I always admired about him. He liked to create spectacular scenarios that highlighted the images behind his fashion on the runway. He always gave his models direction as if we were actors—not just "wear the dress and walk." He always did more. He always directed his girls to perform sharp constructed poses and was the designer who first taught me the couture pose. He proved an amazing stage director—he was very creative, very sharp, very visual, and a perfectionist. Because he was such a visionary, he wanted to create drama when I appeared on the runway, so he envisioned me as a rich diva, a divine, bigger than life, fabulous glamourpuss. He asked me to portray a rich, snobbish woman all jeweled up with big diamonds and other precious stones, a voluptuous, sexy being who's very famous and is always being chased by the paparazzi. Mugler always created amazing scenarios for me and I loved "performing" for him.

Mugler also designed fabulous bustiers for me, constructed from plaster and different materials. One time he molded a plaster bustier in the same color as my skin by forming it around my naked body. To create a dress for the show, leaving portions of the plaster cast visible, he created a dress around the plaster bustier in such a way that it appeared that I was naked. It created the illusion that he was leaving the most curvaceous parts of my body fully exposed, highlighting all the curves. Suddenly this talented, fabulous designer wanted to flaunt my curves and show the voluptuousness of a full-figured woman, to make the large bust and hips a focus instead of hiding them.

That he was showing the beauty of a full-figured woman was fantastic, but the most exciting moment for me was when I sang on the runway, a beautiful song in French, with lyrics that basically said "I'm a doll."

I also felt thrilled and special in 1995 when Mugler asked me to participate in a show celebrating the twenty-year anniversary of his couture house. It was an exceptional show featuring a multi-tiered stage and a combination of all the top models and celebrities like Tippi Hedrin, Julie Newmar, James Brown, and Jerry Hall. It was truly a spectacular visual show. When I appeared in Mugler's show, I received lots of applause. People were going crazy, asking for autographs and taking photographs, making it an incredible experience all over again.

After the show, I continued working with Gaultier and Mugler. Gaultier used me for another ad campaign for one of his collections and Mugler used me for various projects, including the George Michael "Too Funky" video that he directed. Soon I would also be working again with Steven Meisel, when he and Madonna asked me to be a part of her *Sex* book project (more on that in Chapter 2).

A *Size Sexy* Book Is Born

It hadn't dawned on me yet where I was going to go from there or what I wanted to pursue after all these amazing experiences. But the idea for this book, *Size Sexy*, was sparked by a situation that soon followed.

One day when I walked outside after one of the Gaultier shows in Paris, people were waiting for me, which was not unusual, as people often hung around in the hope that they would catch a glimpse of the supermodels, just as they do outside the theater after Broadway shows. In this instance, there were lots of young men and women who ran to me asking for my autograph, asking if they could take a picture with me.

Two young girls approached me, asking for an autograph and a picture. They told me how much they admired me and said they thought it was amazing that I was so big and beautiful—and being allowed to experience this modeling career. Because they were a little bit on the heavier side and French people are not, in general, overweight, they had to deal with all the issues that came with being overweight in Paris. In talking with them, it became very clear that my success was serving as a tremendous inspiration.

I told these young women about my experiences and that I had sworn to myself that nobody, ever, in my life, was going to dictate to me what I should do or make me feel embarrassed about myself or what I do with my body. If anyone tried to control my life or dictate their ideals to me, I would roar at them like a lion.

When I was talking to those beautiful young girls who were asking for my autograph in Paris, it dawned on me: Why were these pretty and curvaceous girls unhappy? Why did they have to go through life with people making them feel bad when they were gorgeous? I realized that these girls looked up to me. They felt I had paved the way for the full-figured girl, ushering in the era of the large-sized woman, helping to illuminate the future for the full-figured girls. Maybe I was a bit ahead of my time, but I was definitely stepping up for all the large women of the world. I was clearing the path for them.

Why I Wrote *Size Sexy*

I figured the only way I could reach a wider public, to clear the path for those girls—and all the many just like them—was by writing a book, this book, so full-figured women throughout the world could share the experiences I have had. My goal has been to help them learn how to deal with the everyday struggles that come along with being full-figured, voluptuous, and curvaceous. I want to show them how to bring out their inner fabulousness, to be reborn with a new confidence and with a new attitude. I want to teach them how to feel inspired, to see the places where I've been, and experience how beautiful I felt. I want full-figured women to know that I felt so gorgeous and secure that the people around me responded to my fabulousness, that they didn't look at me and dismiss me with, "Oh, well she's overweight. She's so big that she's not attractive enough to be a fashion model." I want you, my readers, to understand that the fashion world—the purveyors of what is beautiful in the world—accepted me and even opened doors for me. They loved me and cherished me and wanted to work with me and enjoy my company. They felt inspired by me.

So that era of illuminating the future for the large-sized woman just kept going and growing, and every day, I realized that I had more and more to say, that I was going to say it when the day came, and that day is here.

Why It's Great to Be Me

I'm fierce and fabulous, big and beautiful, smart and sexy, feminine and fantastic, curvaceous and confident, sensual and sultry, and I'm representing this attitude and lifestyle for the big girls, the *Size Sexy* girls!

Throughout this book, I will share the amazing experiences I've had and the enlightening, powerful lessons I have learned about self-love, positive thinking, attitude adjustment, flaunting your assets, and developing and embracing your personal style—all lessons I have collected on my personal journey. Read on to learn more about body image and the many misconceptions that exist in the world about full-figured beauties, and learn how you can become a *Size Sexy* woman too.

chapter **two**

embrace your *size sexy* figure

My wish in writing this book is that it will inspire full-figured women to create a metamorphosis in their own perception of themselves, from feeling big and clumsy to feeling voluptuous and sexy. But before we go on, I want to take some time to explain why I've titled this book *Size Sexy*, and what it means to me.

Crawl Out of Your Cocoon

Size Sexy came to me from my personal experiences as a full-figured woman—from my own femininity, my own sexiness and sensuality. In my eyes, every full-figured woman has the possibility and the right to become a *Size Sexy* woman as well. We are described with all kinds of funky adjectives that are not necessarily complimentary to us as women—some of them may be funny, some of them may be ridiculous—but they do not really describe who we are. They don't describe our sensuality or our generous shape. I decided to break the mold in more ways than one and come up with a much more seductive and attractive name to describe us voluptuous, curvaceous goddesses: *Size Sexy*, because that is what we are.

So, enough of living in a cocoon of constant weight struggles and body issues, of not feeling confident and not living life to the fullest! Lift your head up, look straight ahead, and get out of the bubble, the dark bubble of your weight. Even women who wear a size 2 or 4 or 6 or 10 sometimes think they're big and struggle with their size. But I have accepted the fact that I will never be one of those size 2 or 4 or 6 or 10 women, and I moved past it by deciding to live my life in the best way I could.

Don't misunderstand me: I don't think I'm any different from any other woman who has lived with her weight issues as a constant cloud over her head. I go through my ups and downs with my weight. But, I've decided that my weight will not change my mood or the way I feel about my life. I look good, I take care of myself, I develop my personality, I keep myself fabulous—basically, it's simply about breaking the mold. It's about not caring what other people say or what anyone else's standards are for how women should look and what size we should be and living life according to your own standards; I guide my life according to what makes me happy. As a curvaceous woman, I've been a size 16, 18 . . . and I went up to a size 22 and then came back down to an 18. These are the kinds of weight fluctuations I've always experienced. But it's okay. It's a part of life, as is being happy and self-accepting, feminine and stylish, and having fun with life.

let me tell you!

I have a simple philosophy: I was blessed with this body and this shape, so I will embrace it—wholeheartedly and with gratitude.

Embrace Your Genetics

For most of my adult life, I have been a *Size Sexy* woman. I've always had the tendency to gain weight. The women in my family, on my father's side, are big and curvaceous. I guess I got their genes—the small waist, big hips . . . very shapely, but in voluptuous proportions. My grandmother was a big woman.

She was also a very strong and feminine woman, very much in control, very self-confident, and my aunts, her daughters, were the same way. My aunts all had curvaceous figures and big hips—and they were very outgoing, very sexy, and had very colorful personalities. They passed those traits on to me, while teaching me how to swim and dance. They taught me about life and music and art. My aunts also taught me about belly dancing, a very graceful dance that teaches you to be in touch with your body, how to feel and move confidently. My aunts really taught me a lot about self-acceptance, simply by the way they carried themselves. They were such outgoing, amazing women. My parents were also wonderfully supportive. I received many gifts from all of them, so should I thank them for who I am today? In a lot of ways, I answer with a resounding "yes."

stella's secrets

It's never too late to have a happy childhood! If your childhood was not happy, re-imagine it the way you would like it to be. Envision yourself as loved and accepted and treasured and admired. If you weren't loved enough, love yourself now. Begin by accepting yourself and embracing your *Size Sexy* figure.

My father was a businessman who traveled the world; he inspired me to live life to its fullest. He and my mother filled our home with life and love. My mother was and is one of the most beautiful and glamorous women in the world; she loved to dress up. I got my beauty, sense of style, and outgoing, vivacious personality from her. I have her beautiful blue eyes. My parents also gave me a very active social life. Our home and my immediate family were the center of our whole family's social world. My father and my aunts were singers, full of life, and our house was often filled with live music. I believe the tendency to gain weight came from the genes in that side of the family, because no one in my immediate family has a big figure like I do. My brothers, my sister, I guess they just didn't get those genes—they're average-sized people. But whether I eat a little or a lot, or whether or not I eat rich foods, I always have to struggle with that tendency to gain weight. It's been difficult for me, so I know how other women feel having to go through life dealing with the weight issue.

Which brings me to the reason I'm sharing my *Size Sexy* philosophy with you: I think we should *stop* that struggle, one way or another. When we are born with those genes, with having a tendency to gain weight, that's going to be with us for the rest of our lives. We're going to have to deal with the ups and downs of the scale. Is it fair that we're dealt this burden, those life-long weight fluctuations, when there are other people who don't have the tendency to gain weight, who can eat what they want, whenever they want, and see their weight remain the same? No, of course not, but people have different metabolisms, different genes. That's just the way it is.

But that doesn't mean your weight has to be a controlling factor of your life, and that's what being a *Size Sexy* woman is all about. I don't have a problem with the idea that my weight will likely fluctuate the rest of my life, that I will always be a full-figured woman—I've learned to accept it and embrace it all the way, rather than being unhappy with it and letting it make me a sad, unhappy person.

let me tell you!

Be connected to all those things that make you yourself. If you can do that, your sensuality will arise out of you naturally.

In fact, I like to think that I not only accepted my natural body, but that I took it to another level by embracing it and committing to the idea that my gorgeous, curvaceous figure will serve as a symbol to the outside world of who I am on the inside: an outgoing, vivacious, sensuous, self-confident, glamorous, and feminine full-figured woman who is proud of her body and her mind. And that is what I hope you will take from reading this book—that you, too, will not only embrace your figure, but will take that self-acceptance to another level.

Size Sexy Has Always Been Gorgeous

Throughout history, particularly in the seventeenth and eighteenth centuries, some of the most beautiful women, including nobility, were large women. Their voluptuous figures were seen as a sign of wealth; the rich could afford plenty of food, and all different kinds of it. During the Italian Renaissance, larger women were considered the most likely to produce healthy sons and were thus showered with love and acceptance. There was glory and grace to being a strong, healthy size, unlike today, where women of larger sizes are often made to feel bad about their bodies.

These voluptuous, curvy women were beautiful, so beautiful the greatest artists throughout history chose them as their inspirations. Artists like Picasso, Degas, Renoir, Rubens, Cézanne, and Botero featured shapely women in their masterpieces. For centuries artists have seen curvy women as the epitome of beauty.

In the past, women also donned outfits, like the corset, specifically to show off their curves. Women who were small and shapeless craved the voluptuous figures that some women were lucky enough to sport naturally; so much so they actually laced themselves into tight garments just to give the illusion of having narrow waists, wide hips, and bigger breasts.

And it didn't all grind to a halt after the eighteenth century. Lillian Russell was one of the most popular singers and actresses in the United States in the late 1800s and early 1900s, beloved for her full-figured beauty and gracefulness, as well as her stage presence and mellifluous opera voice. The star, who lived up to the opera diva image by dressing in elaborate, body-hugging corsets, long gowns, and festive hats, also had a reputation for living large off-stage; she and millionaire boyfriend "Diamond" Jim Brady were not shy about enjoying full-course meals in New York City's finest restaurants. (Russell's mother, by the way, was an early feminist—she was the first woman to run for mayor of New York City.)

In the twentieth century, Marilyn Monroe was considered one of the sexiest, most beautiful, most shapely women in the whole world and, by most reports, her weight and dress size fluctuated, supposedly ranging from a size 12 to a size 16. Today, fashion editors and television and film producers crazily think of size 12 as a plus size and size 16 as obese. Nevertheless, in her day, Marilyn's sexy hips and soft curves were legendary and so attractive that powerful men like President John F. Kennedy risked it all to sleep with her.

There were, of course, other women who were vastly admired for their voluptuous figures—Mae West and Sophia Loren, to name a few. And today, we have luscious women like Beyoncé and Jennifer Lopez who are celebrated for their bodacious booties and fabulous bodies. And yet we women are constantly made to feel as if we should be tiny—starving ourselves until we whittle our fabulous *Size Sexy* figures down to a paltry and unattractive size 0! Madness!

fabulous quotes

"Everything I have, I owe to spaghetti."
—Sophia Loren

I mean, are we supposed to ignore these historical precedents and adopt the attitude that these beautiful, shapely figures that have inspired artists, kings, and, yes (I'm the perfect example), even fashion designers are now out of favor? Has the full-figured woman suddenly become less appealing?

The answer is simple: No!

Size Sexy women have not suddenly become less attractive, less fabulous! The fact that women have—and still do—largely dress to show off their curves is proof that we curvy ladies have always been here and have always been appreciated and admired—particularly by men, and if we aren't trying to attract men, then why should we care?

See Yourself as Fabulously Beautiful

Do you know the truth about what is "normal" or "average" or "standard" when it comes to American women these days? Statistically, more than half of all American women wear size 14 or larger. More than half! Additionally, about one-third of all women wear size 16 or larger—and these women look curvy and healthy and sexy. Given those statistics, why are we gorgeous full-figured women the ones who are projected as the odd girls out?

Unfortunately, the images that pepper our lives every day flaunt thin women—very thin women. From billboards and TV shows and larger than life ads on the sides of buses to movie posters and movie stars and ads and articles in nearly every fashion magazine, thinness seems to be prized above all else. These images have been created and hyped by our media and our pop culture.

*fabulous*quotes

"Glamour is what I sell. It is my stock in trade."
—Marlene Dietrich

These super-skinny actresses, models, etc., may occasionally engender politically correct criticisms of their frighteningly thin frames, but their images continue to show up weekly in entertainment and fashion magazines, magazines that clearly continue to hold them up as examples of beauty in Hollywood. The media is just so contradictory with their coverage. One day they criticize these ultra-thin celebrities for being thin-obsessed, and then the next day they put these celebrities back on the covers or plaster their images throughout their magazines. They pay lip service to encouraging healthiness among Hollywood's young women, but then run photos, accompanied by unflattering comments, of any famous woman who dares to put on a few healthy pounds. This waffling on the issue of weight is the very reason we all should look elsewhere for our cues on our bodies, our health, and our self-esteem.

The images that the media perpetuate are constantly changing, so even if you are an "It Girl" one day, the next day you may not be! Never mind that genetics also plays a factor in our weight and ensures that there's no healthy way to constantly try to conform to these changing standards of what is considered the standard for body shape and beauty at any given time! Additionally, the fact that the media attempts to manipulate how we feel about ourselves—and each other—in order to sell magazines masks the dirty little secret that none of those images, literal and figurative, that the magazines are pushing is real.

stella's secrets

I never listen to media hype. The underlying message that the fashion media—and movies, and music videos—keeps sending is: If you're not skinny, you're not sexy. Whoa, hold on a minute. News to the media: That's simply not true! The size of your hips has little to do with sexuality; full-figured women can be—and are—extraordinarily sexy. Make up your own mind. If you feel sexy, you are sexy!

You can trust me when I tell you that many movie stars and models are all beautiful women but not nearly as perfect as they look when they grace the covers of the fashion magazines. Those covers, and the photos inside those magazines, are plotted by a team of makeup artists, hair stylists, and fashion stylists, carefully arranged by photographers and their staffs, and then retouched and manipulated to look perfect by the editorial team at the magazines. All fashion magazines retouch photographs; they lift things, they stretch things, they narrow things, they change positions of legs, and they make body parts seem smaller. In truth, not everything is really as it's shown.

let me tell you!

I found my experiences in the fashion industry to be very inspiring, to women of every size and shape, and I hope that reading this book will help you feel inspired too!

Women don't look like they stepped off the cover of a fashion magazine. Period. Nobody's really perfect—and it's okay. Nobody should dictate how others should live or what size their body should be. You have to believe that your uniqueness makes you superior. You are special.

So why is it that everywhere you look today, full-figured women are bombarded with the message that being a full-figured woman is not what's normal, is not what's in? TV shows and movies are filled with actresses who look like they haven't eaten a carbohydrate in years, models strive to be less than size 0, the larger-sized fashions in most department stores are in the back of the store (or stashed away in a corner on a top or bottom floor), and have you noticed that even some mail in catalogs and websites showcase clothing for full-figured women and have them modeled by thin women? What's up with that? If a catalog is selling full-figured women's clothes, then damn it, they should use full-figured women to model those clothes!

stella's secrets

It's okay to love fashion magazines. Let's be honest: Women on the covers and the inside of fashion and celebrity magazines do look good; they are beautiful. I love my fashion magazines. I live for those spreads and photographs. It is one way to keep up with what goes on with the latest collections and the photographer's works of art. Also, check out the hair, makeup, and accessories in the photo shoots. It is a good source of styling inspiration. Just make sure you don't feel that you have to live up to them, and look at those photos for what they are, while remembering that you are fabulous just as you are. Go ahead and enjoy those magazines; I certainly do!

Kick Those Misconceptions to the Curb

It's time for a revolution, ladies, so let's begin by debunking the myths that abound about *Size Sexy* women. It's time for us to take all those perceptions—misconceptions, really—that people have about full-figured woman and turn them around.

Misconception #1: Full-Figured Women Aren't Sexy

Marilyn Monroe wasn't sexy? Mia Tyler? Jennifer Hudson? Or how about a certain full-figured runway model who was asked to appear in a book called *Sex*? In Chapter 1, I mentioned my appearance in Madonna's famous *Sex* book. After doing several shows with Gaultier, I was approached by Madonna and Steven Meisel for *Sex*. Madonna had asked Gaultier, "Wow, who is this girl? She's amazing, she's sexy, she's beautiful, and I think she would be great in the book." She and Steven agreed that I was perfect for the sex book and, in fact, I was the only full-figured personality in the project.

I flew to New York for the photo shoots for the book, which turned out to be fabulously fun, and turned out some very sexy pictures. In one shot, Madonna and I are in a very sensual position, dressed all in leather and latex, and in a naughty pose. I had stipulated that I wouldn't be photographed in the nude, but Madonna was half naked, and she was spanking me. . . . It was a very erotic situation, which felt wonderful, surreal, and kinky.

I was the only big girl in the book; let's just think about that for a minute. Madonna and Meisel found someone of my size and shape to be beautiful and sexy, and they wanted me to be a part of the most erotic, sensual, sexual, and scandalous book ever published in these modern times. If those amazingly visual people admired and selected someone as voluptuous as me for such a project, then just think about how you should feel about yourself every day.

Yes, *Size Sexy* women, we've got it going on! We'll talk more about our sexiness in Chapter 8, offering up ways for you to embrace your sexy self—and attract men like bees to honey.

stella's secrets

I have always known that my true beauty comes from the inside out. That has helped me express the beauty I possess. I also celebrate the physical beauty that is also part of who I am, and I hope that you will also feel and express both your inner and your outer beauty.

Misconception #2: Full-Figured Women Shouldn't Wear Sexy Clothing

Please! During a 1994 Jean Paul Gaultier runway show, the dress I wore was very tight, showing every curve and shape of my big body. A few days after that show, Paolo Roversi, a well known, talented, and respected photographer, contacted me and expressed a desire to do a shoot with me. That photo shoot went wonderfully. My hair was done and I looked very sensual and very sexy, which is exactly how Roversi wanted to portray me. The way I looked was the way Roversi wanted to represent me because it was the way I represented myself. "You're so beautiful. You're larger than life," Roversi said to me. "You're *divina*," which is Italian for "divine." I felt—and feel—like a sexy voluptuous woman, and that's how I represent myself, including in the way I dress.

We'll discuss ways to strut your stuff in Chapter 4; ways to dress well in Chapter 6; ways to create your own style in Chapter 7; and ways to dress sexy in Chapter 8. Trust me, ladies, if you don't already, you *will* be wearing sexy clothing and feeling great about yourself!

*fabulous*quotes

"I finally realized I don't have to have an A-plus perfect body, and now I'm very happy the way I am."
—Drew Barrymore

Misconception #3: Men Aren't Attracted to Full-Figured Women

To all those people who think *Size Sexy* women are sitting home alone every Friday evening (or any other night of the week, for that matter), let me tell you something. At every size I've been in my life, from size 14 to 16 to 18 to 20 to 22 (and back again), I never had any problems finding men who admired, cherished, complimented, dated, and loved me. Trust me, ladies, I have had *great* romances—and you can too. We're going to talk much more about *Size Sexy* women and romance in Chapter 8, including a game plan to help you find the love of your life.

Misconception #4: Full-Figured Women Are Too Sensitive and Don't Have a Sense of Humor about Themselves

I personally do not get upset about weight jokes . . . if they're funny. I mean, if a joke is funny, even if it's about a full-figured woman or man, I'll laugh, and it doesn't matter if a thin person made it or a large-sized person made it. I don't feel insulted; I won't take it personally.

Part of being a comedian is having the freedom of creation and not having to worry about who might be offended by a joke. I mean, comedians make gay jokes, they make jokes about race . . . they make jokes about everybody. So why should full-figured women be excluded? Why is it wrong if they make fat jokes?

stella's secrets

Taking yourself too seriously is very tiring. Life is beautiful with all its ups and downs, and a sense of humor is necessary. So lighten up ladies and learn how to laugh—even at yourself. It's a million times better than any antidepression pill!

When you hear a good joke, go ahead and laugh; it's okay! As long as it's not meant as a personal attack on someone, it's always okay to laugh at a funny joke. Why not have a good laugh any time you get the chance? Everybody should be able to laugh at herself—skinny, tall, fat, short, whatever your skin color or sexual orientation. It's always good to be able to have a sense of humor about yourself. In fact, my personal favorite *Size Sexy* comediennes are women like Lisa Lampanelli, Mo'Nique, Roseanne Barr, and Dawn French who are funny, smart, talented, and have no problem cracking jokes about themselves.

Misconception #5: Full-Figured Women Should Be Embarrassed to Indulge in Food in Public

Why shouldn't full-figured women enjoy food, whether at home or in public? Who says we can't feel the same passion toward food or cooking or enjoying a good meal as anyone else? I say anyone who questions your right to enjoy food anytime is so off base that there is no reason to listen to anything they say. Rather than feel intimidated, every *Size Sexy* woman should just ignore anyone who is staring at her while she is enjoying her meal. Go ahead and enjoy every sensation, the look, taste, smell, and texture of foods you enjoy.

I'm sure that a lot of women who feel insecure make an extra effort to look and feel sexy and to flaunt their assets and their curves when they go to restaurants and other public places, but if someone gives them a look or they see someone whispering about them, they collapse inside. I understand—but you just have to say, *Who cares what anyone else thinks as long as I'm enjoying myself?* Just remember to keep it in moderation—you don't want to tip the scale.

let me tell you!

I love life; I love to live. I love to eat; I like to indulge. I like my wine. I like to have fun, and I like to be happy—and I don't care what anyone else thinks.

That is what positive thinking is all about, and it's true in everyday life and in every situation. Don't feel insecure! Instead choose to feel fabulous and beautiful and to love yourself no matter what size you are. I mean, that's what I do. Yes, it's true. I have a tendency to gain weight. Am I going to stop enjoying my life? Am I going to stop enjoying food? I love to eat food. I love to eat gourmet food; I do stay away from fast food or junk food, however. I love to try all kinds of food from different countries; I love to cook—I'm a fabulous cook! I got my passion for cooking from my mother and acquired the rest from traveling around the world. I love all those different tastes—it's very sensual. I also entertain and host a lot of dinner parties, which are a great way to enjoy the people in your life while having great food. Like I said, I want to enjoy life, and I have a tendency to gain weight, but since I know that I am beautiful at any size, I allow myself to enjoy my life fully—in public, at the dinner table, and in the bedroom.

These are just a few of the common misconceptions about *Size Sexy* women. See if you can create a list of your own (derived from your family, your community, or your culture's beliefs), and then go through the list one by one and debunk the misconceptions that you know—deep down in your heart—aren't true at all. You'll create spaces for new, healthier, more realistic perceptions about *Size Sexy* women to take root in your psyche and your life.

How's Your Self-Esteem?

In the next chapter, we'll discuss ways that you can bolster your self-esteem and increase your optimism about yourself and your place in the world. But first, take this little quiz to see where you stand on the self-esteem continuum.

How do you describe your appearance?

1. I desperately need to lose forty pounds.
2. I look good, but I weigh more than I'd like to weigh.
3. I have fabulous curves.

How do you treat yourself?

1. I berate myself constantly for being overweight.
2. I am always dieting and never thin enough.
3. I treat myself to my favorite foods and enjoy life.

How do you feel about yourself?

1. No matter how successful I am, if I can't control my weight, I feel like a failure.
2. I have many admirable qualities, but being thin isn't one of them.
3. I'm fabulous and fit and full of life.

How does your weight affect your life choices?

1. I keep waiting for my real life to begin—when I lose the fat.
2. When I lose ten pounds, I'll go on a dating website and also look for a new job.
3. I live my life fully—and I always have.

How do you feel about being a full-figured woman?

1. I would kill to be thin.
2. I like myself, but I'd be a lot happier if I was a size 6.
3. I feel curvy and sexy and very feminine.

Answers

Give yourself one point for each 1 choice; two points for each 2 choice; and three points for each 3 choice.

Score: 5 Someone has burned some very negative images into your poor brain and psyche. You definitely need to shake up your beliefs and bolster your self-confidence.

Score: 5–10 You are still buying into the celebrity and fashion magazine mentality that you need to be thinner. Get ready to loosen up your strictures and fall in love with your sexy body.

Score: 10–15 You're either on the road to a healthy self-image or are already a sexy, confident *Size Sexy* bombshell. Good for you! Read on to celebrate your sexy self.

chapter **three**

create your own reality

Beauty comes in all shapes and sizes and nobody can tell me differently. It's time for the world to both see and accept this. Voluptuous and full-figured women have been loved throughout the centuries, painted by artists, adored by kings, and, more recently, dressed by famous fashion designers. I am the perfect example of that, and I hope my evolution and journey as a confident, voluptuous woman will inspire you. In this chapter, we'll discuss self-esteem and how you can bolster your self-esteem and live your life with increased self-confidence and optimism. And honestly, it begins with the simple act of loving yourself.

Love Yourself Just as You Are

I was never a skinny kid, but I was always happy and positive. Even as a child, I understood the concept of self-love, and I felt very secure. I loved to dance and swim, and I was a very active girl. And even though I was chubby, I didn't accept any negativity or projections about weight issues that people tried to throw my way. I never internalized criticism, never took it to heart, and never went off to hide or feel ashamed. I never felt there was something wrong with me or that I wasn't worthy of enjoying the same lifestyle as everyone else.

I was always the center of attention in my family—positive attention—and I enjoyed it. I was a happy child that used to sing and dance at our numerous family events. And boy! Did we have a lot of them! I was lucky to be surrounded by people who loved me.

let me tell you!

Forty percent of American women wear a size 12 or larger. This amounts to over 65 *million* women. Being *Size Sexy* in Europe is more rare, but I still feel great about my size!

As a kid, my favorite sport was swimming, and I took swimming and diving lessons in a professional lap pool. I would dive from the tallest platforms—headfirst!—and people would often literally stop whatever they were doing to watch me. They would often be amazed that such a young kid was brave enough to do all those high dives, but I was a free-spirited, fearless child.

As a young woman growing up, I was voluptuous, which I have always experienced as sexy and feminine. Basically, at every point in my life, at every weight fluctuation or change in my surroundings, I didn't accept criticism from anyone. I knew I was in charge of who I am, of the things I do, of the way I feel about myself. I decided to embrace and enjoy my life, to be happy with the way I looked, and to celebrate my body, whatever size and shape I happened to be.

That's what made me the woman I am—a confident, bold, sassy, glamorous, and voluptuous *Size Sexy* girl. That's who I am inside, and it's how I present myself to the outside world. That's also what gave me the strength to push myself further than I had dreamed, embarking on a path that would take me to the runways of Paris, being photographed by the most famous and talented photographers in the fashion industry, and into the hands of the most celebrated, brilliant fashion designers in the world.

I know one thing for sure: *Your* perception is *your* reality. You create your own ideal. If you view yourself as fabulous at any size, then you will feel fabulous and enjoy your life—no matter how much you weigh at any moment.

Free Yourself from Negative Beliefs

I go through ups and downs with weight, and it doesn't matter. I call this attitude *freedom of size.* And knowing that I have this freedom from caring about whether my dress size is a 14 or a 22 fills me with self-confidence. My belief: You have to enjoy life no matter what size you are.

Please understand that I am not trying to encourage weight gain by any means—I am not saying that it's okay to weigh 300 or 400 pounds. No matter how much I weigh, I try to keep myself at a comfortable size and that's what I want you to do too. Of course I want you to be healthy, but I also want you to know that self-acceptance is what counts, no matter what size you are. If you are comfortable with your size—and you are healthy—then I say be happy with yourself and enjoy every minute of your life.

stella's secrets

I allow everyone to decide his or her own beliefs and I don't go around trying to convince anybody that they should accept us full-figured women. The important thing is that we accept ourselves. When we accept ourselves, the rest of the world will, too. Or they won't—but then that will be their problem.

Every woman is in charge of her own body and the way she wants to live her life. You have to have self-acceptance even if you're full-figured, if you're staying full-figured, if you're voluptuous and curvy, and if that's the way you want to be. If that's not the way you want to be, lose the weight, change your body, do whatever you want to do with it.

Different people are built in different ways, and different people have different genetics. People come in all shapes and sizes, and we should have the freedom to be those sizes if we so choose. It's for you to decide which lifestyle you want for yourself. And it's most definitely 100 percent up to you to decide to be comfortable with yourself, with your size, and, most importantly, to choose how you feel about yourself and how you will represent yourself to the world.

Believe in Yourself

I know there are some full-figured women out there who are traumatized by certain situations when it comes to going out, looking fabulous or sexy, being confident, living life, and being happy. Maybe their low self-esteem stems from childhood or from other situations they experienced and carry with them, or maybe it stems from letting the media and societal perceptions control how they feel about themselves. For whatever reason, many women don't realize that they should love who they are and appreciate and cherish themselves.

For me, this resolution came from one small experience during my childhood. My family was having a reunion, and we were all gathered around the dinner table. One aunt looked at me and said, in front of everyone, "Oh, you're a little fat! You should start controlling what you eat, eat more yogurt and vegetables." I was very embarrassed that she did it like that, so bluntly, so publicly. I decided then and there that nobody—nobody!—was ever going to talk to me like that or make me feel insecure in any kind of way. And I have kept that promise to myself since that day. That's what came shining through, and that's how I've lived my life ever since.

This belief in myself is what those fashion designers, those people who came to the fashion shows, those famous photographers, and all those people who wanted to work with me in the fashion world saw too. I have always felt good in my own skin, and so all of that was coming out, shining on the runway, in front of the camera, on the pages of fashion magazines. The aura of my walk, the attitude, and the pride I feel were fully present, and no one was going to be able to shake that, to take that away from me.

let me tell you!

Criticism about my body weight is not relevant to me; I simply don't let it penetrate my self-image. Be like me. Embrace that attitude for yourself.

Learning to believe that you are beautiful can be a challenge, because the desire to become a certain shape is often based on somebody else's idea of what a woman should look like. But I am how I am, and you are how you are, and it's all about loving yourself no matter what anybody says. If you're big, you have to be big and proud. And if you cannot believe in your beauty, there are plenty of ways to learn how. I have always felt comfortable in my own body; I relish my size. And I hope you'll learn to feel that way about your body, too.

stella's secrets

I radiate confidence. When you're confident, you project a positive image of someone who is full of optimism and embraces life. On the other hand, if your self-confidence is low, it can mean people see you as someone who is negative, defeatist, and thinks very little of yourself. It's clear which person you should aspire to be, right?

The Uniqueness of You = The Fabulousness of You

You have got it going on no matter what size you are . . . believe that! You have to understand that you can be as sexy, feminine, and sensual as any other woman. And if you accept your differences—and even celebrate them—that makes you not only unique, but fabulous.

We've already talked about how women throughout history have not always been made to feel like outcasts if they weren't a size 2. Quite the opposite, full-figured gals like Mae West, Marilyn Monroe, Lillian Russell, and Catherine the Great were loved for their curvy appearances. And the one thing that all those women—or any woman who has been loved even though she may not fit whatever the current "It Body" is—have in common is that they were full of self-confidence. They knew they had qualities that attracted people to them: These women carried themselves with pride, cultivated a sexy, sensual image of themselves, and projected to the world that that was the way they felt about themselves inside.

Life is too short to treat yourself, or to allow others to treat you, in any other way. Instead, life should be about indulging; it's all about enjoying your life. If you're healthy, you should be happy, you should feel good, and everybody will love you back. When you accept yourself and are happy with yourself, no matter what size you are, that's what you reflect on the outside, and that's the feedback you will get from the world.

let me tell you!

If you love yourself, others will love you in return.

Don't Be a Fraidy Cat: Roar Like a Lion

Personally, I don't care about the rest of the world and what they have to say about my body. In life, it's about how you feel and whether you accept yourself. Ideally, no one would be pressured to conform to standards that other people have set for how they look and wouldn't care if others were happy with the way they look. There is enough pressure in life, just working and walking through our daily routines; we live in a pressure-filled world. So who needs additional pressure about looking a certain way, especially if you simply are not meant to look that way? Not everyone is built like a supermodel and not everyone wants to be, either. We're all shaped differently. I don't have a problem with my shape, and if someone else does, that's about him or her—not about me.

*fabulous*quotes

"Cultivate your curves. They may be dangerous, but they won't be avoided."
—Mae West

I both love and defend my curves—or at least that's what I do when I say I roar like a lion. The lion roars and reveals her claws to protect her cubs. I roar and reveal my nails to protect my curves. Not literally, of course. But when someone has something negative and inappropriate to say to me about my body, when someone tries to shake my foundation with a nasty stare or a whisper, I roar like a lion and I pull my impeccably manicured red nails out to deflect whatever they throw my way, whether it be verbally or visually, by throwing a look right back at them.

Each and every one of us has issues, whether you are big or small. Believe me, even models have issues. As beautiful as they may look, as perfect as their worlds may seem, and as confident as they may act, the smallest thing can shake their foundations. They, just like everyone else, have issues with themselves, with their bodies. But if these models can strut their stuff on the runway, you can learn to love yourself too!

fabulous quotes

"Courage doesn't always roar. Sometimes courage is the quiet voice at the end of the day, saying I will try again tomorrow."
—Mary Anne Radmacher, Inspirational Writer

Reject Size Discrimination

Most of us, unfortunately, have had experiences where people have judged us harshly because of our size or tried to make us feel bad about ourselves. Whispers when you walk into a room, glances and judgmental looks when someone sees a full-figured woman enjoying a rich meal, rude stares from strangers when you enter a movie theater or get on an airplane—even clothing salespeople, whose job it is to help you around the store, sometimes treat large women like creatures from another planet if we dare to browse outside the plus-size sections!

Do you know who serves as our worst criticizer? Believe it or not, it's our own kind—women. What I don't understand is *why* women are the worst criticizers of other women. We are full of negative judgment for one another. In fact, women are even worse than men, because men still find beauty in all sizes and shapes. Women will say terrible things behind your back without knowing you, especially if you are full-figured, have got it going on, and are obviously sexy. They will even have something harsh to say if you're a smaller size. They will talk about the way you look. And have you ever noticed that women will always tell other women that they are fat even if they are clearly not? So ladies, stop hating, and stop being your own worst enemy. And, if it so happens that you see a woman—full-figured or not—who has it going on better than you, maybe you should take notes and admire her fabulousness. There is no need to be so insulting and disrespectful. Don't forget that you, as a woman, are also suffering from that same pressure of society, media criticism, and *sizism*. Try to be more positive and live and let live at large.

stella's secrets

I know how to be sassy—in the best sense of the word. And you can learn too. When you get to the point of accepting your body, don't let any critical remark that someone makes about your weight send you back to where you started. Try being sassy—defend yourself and shoot a remark back at them.

Unfortunately, since there is size discrimination in the world, we'll now discuss ways to deal with it—ways a *Size Sexy* woman can dismiss judgments or criticism and hold onto her confidence.

Don't Let Them Shake Your Foundation

Back when I was asked to participate in a Steven Meisel photo shoot for *Italian Vogue*, I walked into the room where the other models were and got a little look from Linda Evangelista. She was known to be a bit shady and she had such a major attitude because she was a big, big fashion diva. She gave me a bit of a look, with some attitude—not so very welcoming. Someone else might have crumbled. But I thought to myself, "No sweetie. You're not going to make me crumble, because I am here just like you are."

stella's secrets

Strangers are strangers; they're in your life for a short time. So why let what they say get to you? When a stranger makes a negative comment or shoots you a judgmental look, let it bounce right off of you. They don't know you, and any judgment they make about you in that short time is an uninformed opinion.

Later, when I was getting ready to walk the runway in a second collection for Gaultier, I was going through fittings where he was creating another gorgeous corset for me. I felt sexy and amazing. And when it came time to get ready for the show, the excitement was building, and I felt like I belonged backstage. I was sitting in my chair and my dress, with the corset, was hanging in my dressing area. There were two models, a male and a female, sitting there, looking at my dress. It was a gorgeous dress, but compared to their outfits, it was much bigger and it was made up of a lot of fabric. If you put my dress next to the female model's dress, hers would look tiny. So, they were looking at it, and they started giggling to themselves. I could practically read their minds, and knew at once what they were thinking of this big dress, but that was okay. It made no difference to me. I felt incredible to be a part of this show by this incredibly talented designer. Forget them! Gaultier had asked me to walk his runway, and I belonged there every bit as much as they did, and the dress I wore was every bit as stunning as anything worn by the thinner models.

And that's the truth. I was asked to be a part of that runway show and that photo shoot as a model just like all the other models were. I belonged there as much as they did. And that's true for everyone in his or her own life. It is something I want you to remember when others try to make you feel bad, or unworthy, or less than them. You have as much right to go where you want, live where you want, shop where you want, eat where (and what) you want as everyone else does. You have the right to be happy, to live your life, to have the kind of body you want to have, no matter what anyone else says or thinks about it.

You Decide What You *Think*

People are always going to find something to talk about if that's what they want to do. You could be drop-dead gorgeous and the perfect size 2, and if they wanted to find something negative to say, they would assume you must be stupid since you're so beautiful. If you're smart, they'll assume you must not have much of a social life. If you're wealthy, they'll assume you're a snob. If people are determined to be negative, they can find something—or simply make something up!—to say about everybody.

The question is, do you want to live your life based on what other people say? And what about when these people are complete strangers? Think about it: You're sitting with friends, laughing, enjoying each other's company, indulging in a fantastic meal, and someone flashes you a look because you are a full-figured person who dares to be in public partaking of a delicious dinner. In an hour or two, you're probably never going to see that rude stranger again. So are you going to let your lovely evening, your mood, be spoiled because of some ignorant person making stupid comments? No! It's not worth it. Sweetie, just indulge and enjoy!

*fabulous*quotes

"No one can make you feel inferior without your consent."
—Eleanor Roosevelt

Brush It Off

So, that means, ultimately, that the best way to deal with negativity is to not deal with it at all. Let it bounce off of you. Don't internalize the comments people make; do not let the comments become part of what you think of yourself. Laugh them off. When I'm in the company of friends or family, I usually ignore any negativity that comes my way.

stella's secrets

Some people like to play power games by trying to embarrass others about the way they look. I don't play those games. If there's a power struggle and someone is trying to embarrass me, especially when I am feeling beautiful, I will not be the one to look away or cast my eyes downward. If anything, I'll hold their glance and smile at them—make them look down, and most often they do!

However, there are, of course, times when you don't want to simply ignore the negative remark, the glances, or the rude whispers. And there have been times when I haven't ignored the rudeness, when I've turned that person's negativity right back at them. Say I'm at a cocktail party, looking glamorous and sexy, enjoying good food, and someone starts to stare at me, obviously thinking that I, as a large woman, should not be indulging in delicious food. I'm definitely not going to ruin my good time by getting aggravated or angry. But if I want to tease them, mess with them a little, I might continue eating and make faces at them, while proclaiming loud enough for them to hear, "Mmmm yummy, this is so delicious!" Maybe I'll even lick my fingers! I'll make it clear that not only am I eating this food, but I'm enjoying it to the fullest. If I'm in that sassy mood, it's a good way to let them know that I'm having a good time at this party. It's about turning the mirror back at them and letting them see how ridiculous and stupid they're being.

Sometimes just tossing a look—a look full of attitude—back at them is effective. Give them the kind of look that will make them crumble, put their tail between their legs, and feel as embarrassed as they tried to make you feel. However you decide to handle these situations, just remember that you're responding to an action where people have commented on something that's none of their business. It's your life, it's your enjoyment of your life, and it's your body.

*fabulous*quotes

"I believe that it's better to be looked over than it is to be overlooked." —Mae West

Choose Your Words Carefully

Sticks and stones can break your bones, but words can break your confidence. It may seem like a small thing to some people, but I think the phrases and words used to describe large women play a huge role in how we come to think of ourselves. Overweight . . . fat . . . obese . . . chubby . . . all of those words may be accurate, and some of them are even legitimate medical terms, but how do they make you feel when you hear them? Think about the words you would use to describe your body, your size, your shape to someone. Would any of those words be on your list?

Positive Words

These are words that describe us larger ladies without insulting us. Choose the ones that leave you feeling good and use them in your conversations.

- Full-figured
- Voluptuous
- Curvaceous or curvy
- Buxom
- Shapely
- Well-developed
- Zaftig
- Rubenesque

Negative Words

These are the words that you don't want to use when talking about yourself. Eliminate them from your vocabulary and don't allow others to use them in your presence either.

- Obese—I know it's a medical term, but part of the Dictionary.com definition of the word includes the phrase "grossly overweight," and who wants to be thought of as "grossly" anything? I resent this word!
- Puffy
- Overweight—over what weight? Who determines this weight that we're "over"?
- Plump
- Portly
- Pudgy
- Stout
- Rotund
- Corpulent
- Outsized—Again, out of what size?

As I said, it may seem like a small thing, but you have the power to decide which words you use, and therefore which words you perpetuate the use of. So it's worth taking the time to choose your words carefully.

let me tell you!

There are so many women who weigh 135 or 145 lbs. or less who walk around saying, "I'm so fat." These girls are not fat and it's ridiculous that pressure from society and the media makes them feel as though they are. It is just so ridiculous for these women to refer to themselves as fat simply due to the influence of the media! They have their own type of beauty and need to own that. Their insecurities are all in their minds.

So What If You're *Size Sexy* and Pregnant?

Some women have issues about their bodies when they are pregnant or after they give birth. If this sounds like you, I think you need to change your perspective. All you need to think about is making sure that both you and the baby are healthy. Again, pressure from society and the media makes women feel almost guilty and scared that they will gain weight while they are pregnant instead of just allowing them to enjoy that fabulous experience and not worry about that pair of jeans that they are not going to fit in for a while, or maybe not ever again depending on their body type. During pregnancy, some women hardly gain any weight and some gain a lot more. You have others who lose some of the weight and others who keep some. I'm sure there are husbands who put pressure on their wives for gaining weight, but you should tell them that if they have a problem with it, they can carry the next baby. We are not mannequins. At the same time I am not advocating that you let your weight get out of control either, but women's bodies go through a lot of changes, especially when changing hormones are involved.

I recommend the same confident *Size Sexy* attitude for women I like to call "Pregnant Beauties." If you're *Size Sexy* and pregnant, celebrate your beauty and take care of yourself. Be a well-groomed, healthy pregnant lady. This is not the end of your beauty. It is just going through another phase. Make sure you bring back the romance into your home and bring back that sexy attitude. Don't neglect your man while you're pregnant. I'm sure that with a lot of creative alternatives and the help of a few good books that won't be a problem.

After you give birth you may still be carrying that baby fat; that will take some time to lose and you should deal with it by making some positive changes. Begin with a change of attitude toward yourself. Stop putting yourself down or worrying and start accepting and understanding what your body is going through. If this seems impossible, just look at your wonderful bundle of joy and you will instantly remember that your baby is worth every extra inch you have gained on your body. Keep yourself pampered and create a new style. Don't hide behind big and frumpy clothes. Accept the fact that you can still be a hot mama with your new body and with that miracle right next to you—and know that hot mamas come in all shapes and sizes.

How's Your *Size Sexy* Attitude Coming Along?

Now that we have talked in depth about ways a *Size Sexy* woman can choose to feel good about herself and dismiss those who seek to put her down or rain on her parade, we are ready to move on to ways a *Size Sexy* woman can strut her stuff. Before we go, however, I want you to take a moment to ask yourself what you have learned from the last two chapters. Are the following *Size Sexy* tenets your new beliefs?

1. Being *Size Sexy* can be positive.
2. Being the shape you are makes you unique, and unique can be fabulous.
3. It doesn't matter how others see you. What matters is how you see yourself.
4. Negative people are lost in their own ignorance and you can absolutely roar back at them if they are rude.
5. You should ignore size discriminators and surround yourself with *Size Sexy* admirers.
6. People will always talk, no matter what size or shape you are, so therefore, let them talk.
7. We women have to stop being each other's enemies and support each other positively when it comes to our looks.
8. Success and talent can definitely be achieved, even if you are a *Size Sexy* woman.
9. Freedom of size is the new attitude because there is more to you than your size.
10. *Size Sexy* women really are everywhere.

If you are good to go on these underlying truths, then you are on the right path. If you're still not a true believer, hold steady and keep reading. You'll get there eventually!

chapter **four**

strut your stuff

What matters most, my fellow *Size Sexy* women, is to feel good about yourself. You have to be happy in your own skin and know that you're beautiful and that you have a lot to offer, just like anybody else. Always remember that this size that you are, this body that you have, is beautiful. If you truly believe that, it will be reflected on the outside, and others will see your beauty, too.

Attitude, Attitude, Attitude—Get Some!

When you approach your life with a positive attitude, it means you are seeing everything in the right way. When you project a positive attitude, it shows that you are in control both of yourself and of your surroundings.

Being positive and projecting a positive attitude goes hand in hand. The fact is, when you're positive, you've accepted yourself. But it's important to not only be positive, but to let that positivism show to the outside world. That's where attitude really comes in.

When you can successfully project a positive attitude to others, it shows them that you have strength, self-control, and self-acceptance, that nothing will make you feel insecure (because you won't allow it!). We have discussed a lot of the basics in the previous chapters and are now ready to discuss ways that you can project your positive, *Size Sexy* attitude to the world.

let me tell you!

You set the mood that colors your life. Let it be a sunshiny day every day when it comes to your self-acceptance.

Be Unique

Remember that no one is built the same way genetically, and that's why we're not all the same shape. But the differences are what make you unique. Make the most of what makes you special and celebrate your individuality. Who wants to be just another stick-thin girl?

Start Now

Don't wait until you are a certain size to lead a happy, productive life. Life goes by very fast, and there are so many things to do and accomplish. As soon as you've finished reading this book for fortification and ideas, you will understand that *now* is the time to start living your life to the fullest. No more waiting—live now.

Open Your Eyes

They say that beauty is in the eye of the beholder. Sure, it's a cliché, but it's true. It's also true that your eye should be the first one opened to seeing your beauty. If you truly see and truly accept your beauty, the rest of the to-be beholders will follow. See yourself as you are: fabulous!

Find Yourself

Everyone needs validation that they are special in this universe. Watch movies with strong, beautiful female characters of different sizes and shapes, women who will inspire you. See Chapter 10 to get ideas as to what movies to watch.

Dress for Success

If you have been wearing baggy, shapeless, dull clothes, splurge on clothing that makes you look and feel feminine and sexy. It's a fabulous and fabulously fun way to boost your self-confidence—and you deserve it!

Lighten Up

Stop being so hard on yourself. As Mae West says, "I never loved another person the way I love myself." And to me, that means a lot. You only have yourself to live with. Accept it by loving yourself a little more.

Love Your Body

Start acting as if you love, and have always loved, your body. No matter what size or shape you are, your body is your temple, your home, and as a result, it will empower you to make the change. You'd be lost without that beautiful body, so show it how much you love it by celebrating its fabulousness.

Change Your Mindset

Learn to recognize people around you who are size discriminators and disregard their attitudes. Create your own positive ideals about who you are and how you look. Your attitude is the only attitude that really matters.

Look for Ways to Express Your Uniqueness

Clothes and accessories are marvelous ways to bolster your image. Accept your body and develop your own, distinct, sexy, feminine style to show it off. We'll discuss lots of ideas for developing real style in Chapter 7.

Be All That You Can Be

Stop being obsessive about your weight. It is not all that you are. You know the qualities of your inner self whether it's your personality, talent, intelligence, or creativity. Take the focus off your body and focus on the qualities that make you an interesting person to know and love.

stella's secrets

In life, when a good opportunity comes my way, I go for it. When the opportunity to work with the fashion world's top designers, photographers, and models came my way, I took it, embraced it, made it even bigger, and had fun with it. So don't be afraid to be a self-confident *Size Sexy* woman and take advantage of the opportunities that will come your way. When they do, trust that you'll know how to make the most of them!

Who Says You're Fabulous? You!

If you let it, a positive attitude will become your reality, something you'll use every day of your life in terms of your body, your shape, your looks, and your self-acceptance.

A positive reality is what my attitude is for me every day, when I get dressed, when I interact with people, and when I walk down the street. This is something that must become a part of your life, too, if you want to be happy with the *Size Sexy* person that you are. It's something that you have to make a part of your life; no one else can do it for you.

And if you don't, or you can't, view who you are and how you look in a positive light, then make the changes necessary to get you to that place. I don't encourage anyone to remain unhappy with themselves; in fact, quite the opposite. If you think making a change will make you happy, whether it be with your weight, your hair, your clothing, your makeup, your outlook on life, or some other aspect of your personality, then that's what you have to do.

I don't know if our society can get to a place where everyone is accepted and admired, whatever their size. But I do know that if you're secure with yourself and if you're content with yourself, then it won't matter what other people say or what other people think. People will always find negative, vindictive, offensive things to say if that's the kind of people they want to be. And it's up to you to decide how, or if, you'll deal with it. I recommend being confident, deflecting their ignorant opinions and just kicking them to the curb or bouncing those opinions right back at them.

let me tell you!

You only have one life, so live it to the fullest and make yourself happy.

Bring the Inside Outside

The key to presenting a confident, positive self to the outside world is *being* a confident, positive person, so accept yourself, and own your behavior toward yourself and other people. Instead of spending all your time worrying about your body, why not spend your time and efforts trying to change others' attitudes toward you? Their negativity is basically due to size discrimination. But, if you show them that you are happy and have a positive attitude toward yourself and your beauty, you're showing them the defining characteristics of a *Size Sexy* woman. Remember, you don't fall apart, in any situation, ever. It just should not be a part of your makeup. The minute people see that you are a vivacious, self-confident, and gorgeous being, they will have to replace their misconceptions about the *Size Sexy* female. And this will all come from you shining your light!

let me tell you!

I believe in shaking the world, or at least the ideas of those who are around me. I really want to abolish negative misconceptions about size, weight, and sex appeal.

Talk the Talk

Now that you are gaining in confidence, it's time for you to learn how to talk the talk and live your life as a *Size Sexy* woman. If you are a shy or nervous person, the following suggestions, a few extra morsels of food for thought, will help you as you create your *Size Sexy* talk.

Go Out into the World

No more sitting home alone. A *Size Sexy* woman is not a shy, retiring flower. Make sure you interact with others. You must first believe in yourself before others will believe in you, but you'll solidify your feelings of confidence when you see how well people respond to your positive, self-confident self.

Take the Focus Off Your Size

When you are out in the world interacting with others, you need to avoid focusing on weight; instead, being a *Size Sexy* woman is about projecting your personality. Build your power from within by letting all of your amazing inner qualities shine through. Let people see your real personality and everyone will be looking into your eyes and not at your thighs.

*fabulous*quotes

"I can't understand how a woman can leave the house without fixing herself up a little, if only out of politeness. And then, you never know, maybe that is the day she had a date with destiny, and it's best to be as pretty as possible for destiny."
—Coco Chanel

Be Bold

If your usual mode is to hang back, stand in the corner not talking to anyone, or fade into the wallpaper, force yourself to do something new—talk to someone, anyone! Don't be afraid to approach *anyone.* No one is perfect and no one is better than you!

Dress for the Occasion

Make sure you're dressed appropriately for whatever the occasion you're attending. Being confident in how you're presenting yourself allows you to be confident period. Plus, when you spend time thinking about your clothing and appearance, you are more likely to feel as if you're worth it—and you are!

Make an Impression

Don't be afraid to stand out in the crowd. That may sound ridiculous, but people can often be so afraid of judgments or negative reactions that they're afraid to do anything that will get them noticed at all. So again I say, don't be afraid to have fun and stand out with your fabulous self!

Look Them in the Eyes

Eye contact is a must. No exceptions! Just think about how charming and forthright you find others to be when they are confident enough to make eye contact with you. Don't you want people to find your ability to make eye contact charming and forthright?

stella's secrets

I always make eye contact. Because when you meet someone's eyes directly, it's a sign of respect. It shows the person you're conversing with that you are paying attention to what they're saying and that you're truly engaged in chatting with them.

Don't Sweat the Small-Minded

You are smart and sassy—harsh judgments or negative reactions simply do not come your way. Either kick them to the curb or let them float right over your head. Remember, you have a lot more going on than just your size. Besides, you're wonderful!

Be Fabulous

Self-esteem, confidence, and putting forth the impression that you are a vibrant, sexy, social being are contagious. People will be attracted to you and ask themselves, "Who is this amazing woman?" Keep practicing these tips and you will have nothing to worry about; you will become the *Size Sexy* woman who is the life of the party.

*fabulous*quotes

"Reality is a world as you feel it to be, as you wish it to be, as you wish it into being."
—Diana Vreeland, Former *Vogue* Editor and Style Icon

When You Fall Down, Pick Yourself Right Up Again

No matter how hard we work to build our self-esteem, we all have those days when we don't feel good about ourselves. Even thin girls get the blues, so don't start thinking that you only have bad days because you're bigger than other girls. You must know what a waste of time it is to think those kinds of ridiculous thoughts. When you feel blue, or discouraged, what you need are ways to pick up your spirits. Here are a few quick pick-me-up tips:

1. Go to a clothing store that carries your size and buy a couple of daring outfits that you never had the courage to wear until now. Experiment with something a little sexier, a little more outstanding, or a little tighter and stand in front of the mirror to see how fabulous you can look. Remember, you always look better dressed up than dressed down.
2. Love yourself unconditionally. That means with no conditional requirements, such as being twenty pounds lighter.
3. Say to yourself, "I want to become a stylish girl" and know that you can.
4. Realize that it is time to stop the weight drama, and then do just that.
5. Repeat this daily: "I am acknowledging and beginning to admire my shape."
6. Take this vow: "I'm going to stop hating my body immediately."
7. Don't wait for the party to come to you. Become more of a socializing personality and bring the party to them.

8. Start understanding the fact that it is not only possible but also time for *you* to become flirty and feminine.
9. If you're nervous talking to someone, say to yourself over and over again, "I am smart and intelligent and can hold a conversation about anything."
10. Stop minimizing yourself. There is nothing minimal about you.

If you have practiced all these quick pick-me-up tips and feel ready, then step out into the big world with big happy steps.

stella's secrets

I'm a proactive girl, and I want you to be one too. When you are feeling bad about your self-image to the point where you are unhappy, be strong and take action. Say "Enough of that. Time to make a few changes!" Decide which changes will uplift and improve the way you see yourself and then do whatever is necessary to make them happen. Happiness will be your friend in no time.

Walk the Walk

Projecting a healthy, sassy *Size Sexy* attitude can come from the way you stand or the way you talk to others. In general, it's about the way you carry yourself. When I say you've got to walk the walk, I'm speaking literally. A sexy walk means incorporating all your assets—your femininity, your sensuality, your self-acceptance, your attitude—into one attention-grabbing sashay. It's about presenting a positive visual of what a *Size Sexy* woman is and saying to the world, "Yes, I am big and beautiful, and I am big and proud . . . get it?" That—putting the whole package of your looks, your attitude, your personality, your confidence, and your sexy state of mind into a move that will turn heads—is what a sexy walk is all about, so walk that walk girl!

This is the package that each *Size Sexy* woman should develop for herself. Everything starts from here, so gather these great things from within yourself and project them to the outside world. Once you have all that going on, believe me, the confident posture and the sexy walk will come together quickly.

Just remember, it all comes from within. And if you don't have it all together now, by the time you're done reading this book, you will!

Sexy Is as Sexy Does: How to Walk the Sexy Walk

It's all about attitude, ladies. So why settle for an ordinary walk when you can wow them with a *Size Sexy* strut? If your attitude needs a booster shot, here are the steps to get your motor humming:

1. You've got to have the sexy, self-confident attitude before you can turn it into the sexy, self-confident walk. It all begins with the attitude!
2. Don't forget that the eyes—and eye contact—are part of the experience.
3. If it's tough to conjure up the attitude, the spirit of the sexy walk, from within, look to a famous sexy woman whose figure and attitude and sex appeal inspires you. In my case, it's all about old Hollywood: Marilyn Monroe in *Some Like It Hot* (or any of her movies), Jayne Mansfield in *The Girl Can't Help It*, and Sophia Loren in all of her films. And for a more recent example, there's supermodel Naomi Campbell, who is best known for the way she swings her hips down the runway. Be inspired by these fabulous women.
4. Now, when it comes to creating the walk itself, take a deep breath, put your chin up and breasts slightly forward, and carry yourself as tall as possible. Don't hunch. Imagine there is a straight line in front of you. Be light on your feet. Wiggle your waist a little, but don't wiggle it too much. Keep your motion in proportion to the rest of your walk; in other words, don't overdo it. Most importantly, to get into that swing you should be rocking a pair of gorgeous high heels.
5. Remember, don't walk like a bulldog; carry yourself like a graceful panther.

Find Role Models to Inspire You

To all the curvy goddesses out there, we shouldn't have to wish we lived in an environment of old-world beauty where we would be prized for our voluptuous shapes. But we should understand and always remember that curvy goddesses were held in high esteem in the past, for hundreds of years, and that's the way it *should* be now. We must learn to love and accept our beauty, and then others will see our true beauty and will love us—just as we are—too.

One way to increase your self-confidence and self-esteem is to find role models that will inspire you to enjoy your fabulousness. For some, it's encouraging to have a role model, and if you find one, it can be a very important part of building a positive outlook and a positive self-image. Everyone feels good when someone with whom they have things—big things—in common does well.

Any woman can become a good role model. Confident, talented, smart, stylish women who take good care of themselves will always draw our attention and inspire us to do the most with the talents we have. My wish for every woman is that, by the time you finish reading this book, you will have found someone who helps inspire you to live your life to the fullest and that you become that kind of role model for someone else, too.

let me tell you!

I have had many fabulous fashion moments as I shared the stage with the world's top supermodels and strutted down the runway with style and grace. A few of the supermodels this *Size Sexy* girl shared the runway with include:

Tyra Banks
Christy Turlington
Linda Evangelista
Cindy Crawford
Naomi Campbell
Claudia Schiffer
Kate Moss
Amber Valletta
Shalom Harlow
Eva Herzigova
Nadja Auermann
Jerry Hall

Elizabeth Cady Stanton, an American feminist and social activist, for example, was one of the first ladies of the American women's rights movement. And in case you did not know, she was a brilliant, bright, strong, full-figured woman. Today, we have role models like Oprah Winfrey, a strong, intelligent, and powerful woman who is admired by millions for her achievements in producing, publishing, and acting, and for her extensive charity work.

stella's secrets

Role models are important, but don't compare yourself to anyone, even positive role models. You are the only you there is. Decide how you want to live your life, and if you are truly content with the result, your reward is that you'll become a role model to others.

Legendary Divas

There are several incredible, talented, strong, beautiful, and inspiring full-figured women from the past that I personally admire. Here are a few:

Sophie Tucker

She was a singer and a comedienne who played piano and sang burlesque and vaudeville tunes during which she emphasized her big size with humor and sexuality. She sang songs with amazing titles, which had to do with her size, such as, "I Don't Want to Be Thin" and "Nobody Loves a Fat Girl but Oh How a Fat Girl Can Love." One of her most famous songs was "My Yiddishe Momma," a song she wrote for her mom.

Ella Fitzgerald

Fitzgerald was a truly talented and fabulous jazz singer, also known as Lady Ella. She was a full-figured woman who reigned as the most popular female jazz singer in America. The audience did not care about her size. They simply fell in love with her voice, and I feel the same way. She was amazing!

Mahalia Jackson

She was a big woman with a big voice and a big soul who many considered the queen of gospel music. She once said she weighed 200 pounds, but with her good Louisiana cooking, her weight could shoot up to 240 pounds. Ms. Jackson was my kind of girl. She was so happy that you could hear it in her amazing singing voice.

Contemporary Ladies

We don't have to look to the past to find role models; there are plenty of modern women who are big, beautiful, and successful. A few I admire include:

Kathy Bates

Kathy Bates is a talented actress who has won several awards and an Oscar for her phenomenal and impressive acting career, but what is more impressive is that she was over forty and a full-figured woman when she won breakthrough opportunities and made a splash in Hollywood, a town that does not typically accept, let alone admire, women of a certain age and size.

Queen Latifah

Who doesn't love the Queen? She's a very talented woman who's got it going on in several different fields. Whether it's music, acting, or being a spokesperson for cosmetics lines, she always projects self-confidence. And, even though she has been a spokesperson and advocate for Jenny Craig, she's never seemed to have any problem being comfortable with her weight, showing up on the red carpet at award shows in gowns that are every bit as beautiful and figure-hugging as thinner women. And, as for her Jenny Craig program, if *she* decided that she wanted to put herself through a change, then fine; I've always said, if you're not happy with the way you are, then you should definitely make a change.

Camryn Manheim

Camryn Manheim is another talented woman and actress who happens to be full-figured. She has lost weight in recent years, but again, if that's something that was important to her based on her own decisions and opinions about her body or her health, that's great. It just goes to show you that it's possible if you want to. It's all about how you feel about yourself.

Jill Scott

She is a voluptuous and very talented woman who has an incredible voice and stage presence. Scott makes wonderful, happy music and never appears to have a problem with her weight. To me, she is quite sexy and marvelous.

fabulous quotes

"It's so reassuring to have a woman heroine who triumphs with more than just what she has on the outside . . . who has more to offer the world than just a pretty picture. To me, the tragedy about this whole image-obsessed society is that young girls get so caught up in just achieving that they forget to realize that they have so much more to offer the world."
—America Ferrera

Jennifer Hudson

She may not have been officially crowned the *American Idol,* but she believed in herself and her talent and went on to show her beauty and unmistakable star quality to the entire world. Winning an Academy Award was just the beginning of this diva's life as a superstar—and she always looks absolutely fabulous.

America Ferrera

They had to resort to braces, ugly glasses, and ridiculous clothes to make this stunning actress appear "ugly" on *Ugly Betty*. America is the epitome of a young, healthy, curvy, attractive young woman—and she's ultra-talented too!

She starred in a wonderful movie called *Real Women Have Curves*, which is all about a young woman learning to embrace her body and beginning a successful career. America always looks fabulous on the red carpet.

Adele

A newcomer I adore is British pop star Adele, who has a great voice. She's also self-assured, sassy, amazingly talented, and curvy—very curvy. She frequently wears miniskirts onstage and does so with such confidence. And she's only nineteen, which goes to show you what a great attitude she has about herself to have that much self-acceptance at such a young age. In an interview, she was asked if she was received differently in America than she was in Europe, and her response was that everyone in the music industry tries to reinforce the Hollywood image of thin figures as the ideal. But Adele has said that she will not lose weight unless it becomes a health problem. She's someone I think you should all look to when you have those shaky moments.

Mo'Nique

She's sassy and sexy and has brilliant comedic timing—a star in her own right. I like the fact that she's not afraid to poke a little fun at herself and her size. And she has a handsome husband who apparently adores her and finds her very sexy, so good for her!

fabulous quotes

"FAT means fabulous and thick, full and tasty, fluffy and tender."
—Mo'Nique

Beth Ditto

A singer in the band Gossip, Beth Ditto is already a rock star legend. I find her amazing. She is so comfortable with her body that she sometimes performs while wearing shorts or simply her underwear. She is a very talented young woman, who truly believes that bigger is better. She weighs 230 pounds and is very proud of it; she doesn't give evidence of even one ounce of shame.

I think she is a great inspiration for young women who are intimidated by their weight. She's only twenty-eight years old and doesn't care what other people think; she's a very free-spirited kind of girl. I love her and her *Size Sexy* attitude. She's my kind of girl!

Dawn French

Dawn French is a British actress, writer, and comedienne, who cowrote the ingenious and successful comedy show called *French and Saunders*. Alongside her comedy partner, Jennifer Saunders, Dawn is an intelligent, funny, big, talented girl. She refuses to diet and once said, "If I had been around when Rubens was painting, I would have been his fabulous model. Kate Moss? Well, she would have been the paintbrush." As far as I'm concerned, she is a funny genius, who has hysterically spoofed famous females such as Britney Spears and Catherine Zeta-Jones.

Beyoncé

Beyoncé is not really a large woman, but she is, however, a fabulous role model for all women. Even though she is well rounded, with big thighs, she is incredibly beautiful and knows it—and apparently a lot of men agree. She has a big voice, and a big behind, which she shakes very well. And I love watching her on stage shaking her curves.

fabulous quotes

"It is easy for me to gain weight. I'm not naturally stick thin. . . . I'm not heavy, but I'm not skinny either."
—Beyoncé

And More!

Other full-figured women who are role models for *Size Sexy* women:

- Jordin Sparks
- Kathy Najimy

- Emme
- Marissa Jaret Winokur
- Sara Ramirez
- Mia Tyler
- Kate Dillon
- Nikki Blonsky

I think you catch my drift, that these are just a few of the many big-sized, full-figured, gorgeous, talented women who accepted their size and did not let it be an obstacle on their way to the top. I take off my hat to these beauties. These talented women serve as marvelous inspiration, not just for us full-figured women, but for women of all shapes and sizes that have issues with their bodies.

stella's secrets

Make a list of *Size Sexy* women you admire and post it on your wall so you'll wake up every day knowing that *Size Sexy* women like you are fabulous!

How Do You Really Feel about Your Body?

Maybe you thought we would never directly address your body, but you would have been wrong. Why shouldn't we address your body? In my opinion, full-figured women have beautiful, curvaceous bodies that they—and others—have every reason to admire. But before we move on to the next chapter, take the following quiz to see where you stand in relation to body consciousness.

I think my body is . . .

1. An embarrassing encumbrance, something I have to lug around.
2. Heavier than it should be, but healthy and reasonably attractive.
3. A feminine wonder to behold—curvy, soft, voluptuous, and lovely.

My relationship with my body has always been . . .

1. Distant, as if it were not even attached to my personality.
2. Friendly, we kind of go together, even if it embarrasses me at parties.
3. Lovely, we have a fabulous time together, living a fabulous life.

How do you nourish your body?

1. I'm not quite certain what you mean by nourish?
2. I eat lots of peanut butter because my body loves peanut butter.
3. I make special efforts to eat food that meets my body's need for nutrients.

How often do you exercise?

1. Does walking from my house to my car count as exercise?
2. I'm not big on exercising, but I take my dog for walks several times a week.
3. I love to move my body so I take long walks two days a week, swim two days a week, and take dance classes whenever my schedule allows.

What do you see when you look in the mirror naked?

1. I try not to see myself naked. Mirrors are not my friends.
2. I see some things that I'm not happy with, but I think I look okay as a whole.
3. I see a beautiful, full-figured woman who loves who she is, inside and out.

Answers

Give yourself one point for each 1 choice: two points for each 2 choice; and three points for each 3 choice.

Score: 5 You're in need of some serious navel-gazing, as in looking down to realize that you have a body and that it might have some needs. Girl, you need to read on.

Score: 5–10 You have some body consciousness, but I suspect it's limited to those zones you think look pretty good, like your calves or your hands. You need to make friends with your whole body and take it on a date or something.

Score: 10–15 You're our golden girl, but I'll wager that we'll have ideas and tips that will help you fall farther in love with your body and become even more fabulous.

chapter **five**

treasure your body and mind

Just like everyone else on the planet, we full-figured women need to acknowledge, accept, appreciate, and attend to our bodies. Our bodies are the vehicles that carry us through life, our longtime traveling companions, the temples of our soul. While I don't advocate dieting unless your health requires you to lose weight, or *you* desire a trimmer figure, I encourage making healthy choices most of the time and keeping yourself active. To help you take this step, we'll open this chapter with words to inspire you to appreciate yourself, and then offer information on ways you can best nourish, protect, and take care of your temple.

Appreciate Your Body

If you are a *Size Sexy* woman who has struggled with weight your whole life and who is finally comfortable with the weight you are, don't let anyone tell you anything different. Absolutely no one! Consider yourself beautiful inside and out. Obviously your outside beauty is based on looks and physicality, but you are the one who sets those standards for what is attractive—no one should set them for you but yourself. You're the one who should feel comfortable and seductive in your body.

These positive feelings about your body all come from self-acceptance. When you accept yourself for who you are, everything else will just follow. From self-acceptance you will have confidence and confidence will help you show your beauty to the outside world. Self-acceptance means allowing yourself to feel and be gorgeous and great, and to be happy with who you are and how you are shaped. Just don't aspire to any images that you know you can't live up to, and things will take care of themselves from there.

Stifle Judgment

The media, for instance, is definitely not the place to go to for your cues about how you should look, unless you are willing to try to live up to their constantly changing standards. But why should you have to contend with those expectations and follow those shifting trends? You should be true to yourself, true to your size. Let everyone know how fabulous you are. Ignore the naysayers. And that's projecting a positive attitude. That's being a *Size Sexy* woman who's happy, who takes care of herself, and who carries herself in the most feminine and attractive way.

Once you learn to project a positive attitude, you will have no problem communicating with people. You will realize that people are open to other people who are interesting, whatever their size. Sure, you will always have people who are judgmental and critical of you, no matter what. But when you present yourself as a strong, confident woman, others have no choice but to respect and embrace you the way you are and for who you are.

fabulous quotes

"If nature had intended our skeletons to be visible it would have put them on the outside of our bodies."
—Elmer Rice, American Playwright

Be Yourself

I went into the fashion industry—an industry full of skinny models—exactly as I was. I was right in the middle of an industry full of all these media images we were just talking about, and yet I was praised and received with open arms. Why? Because of the way I carry myself, my attitude, my positivism, my sexiness, my personality, my femininity, and beauty—and they embraced me. I felt just like one of the girls and they accepted me fabulously with hugs and kisses. We hung out together backstage and we talked and laughed as we got our hair and makeup done together. We also partied together and socialized at many events.

If I were shy and had low self-confidence, that may never have happened. But it is all about what you project to the world, and I showed off my big size and beauty with confidence, just like the other models showed off their small sizes and beauty with confidence. That should speak to each and every *Size Sexy* woman out there, no matter what field you work in. It will happen for you, too.

My hope for each of you is that your own self-confidence will become so obvious that other women will look at you and say that they wish they could be that confident. Other curvaceous women will say that they wish they had the confidence to look like you and carry themselves the way you do. Love and appreciate your body and you, too, can be a role model to others.

Find Ways to Show Your Appreciation

We each have our own ways of pampering ourselves, but often those ways may not include activities or pleasures that feel good to your body. While we, as women, may be focused on fulfilling our needs and desires or experiencing our feelings, we often neglect our bodies and mind. Do you remember how long it has been since you embraced, pampered, and released yourself from your daily stress?

Here are some practical and simple ideas to help you give yourself the appreciation and value that both your body and mind deserve.

Make an Appointment for a Massage

All of us live with responsibilities and deadlines and ongoing pressures to perform, and all of our bodies clench up when tension in our lives becomes commonplace. Massage is a great way to de-stress your body and your emotions. And nothing feels better than a massage when your neck or back aches or your muscles are so tight that balls of knots form just below the surface. Today, there are many types of massage, from gentle stroking to deep-tissue or hot-stone massages. If you're ready to offer your body the gift of stress relief, check out Chapter 9, where we discuss spa treatments.

Take a Walk

Walking is a wonderful way to give your body some light exercise and to relax. When your body feels tired or stressed, take it on a lovely walk around your neighborhood or through a park, stopping here and there to soak in the surrounding beauty and to breathe in fresh air.

Take a Warm Bath

There is nothing as delicious as a warm bath. If you are tired or stressed or feeling down, pour your favorite perfumed oil or bath salts into the tub, put a towel or pillow behind your neck, lie back, and relax. Many essential oils, such as lavender, have proven stress-reducing qualities and are known to promote restful sleep. For increased pleasure, light candles and play soothing music—yes, even when alone! It will help you relax and unwind.

Listen to Music

Music helps us relax. Pick your favorite songs or try a new sound that will take you to a different place, pour yourself a glass of wine (or whatever nourishes you and feels like a treat), light a candle, lie back, and allow the mellifluous sounds to flow over your weary body. Dive in to the sound and allow yourself to de-stress and enjoy.

Meditate

Meditation is a great way to discover peace within yourself and to relax your body and mind. It can also help you improve your concentration and increase your happiness, and will definitely help reduce stress and anxiety. There are many levels and techniques that you can learn in a workshop and at local centers.

Read a Good Book

Buy or borrow a book on any subject you find interesting, as long as it captivates your imagination and takes you on a long journey to a different place. The idea is to have it disconnect you from the current reality.

Discover a New Hobby

Hobbies can be beneficial for self-balance and harmony. They can provide an outlet for stress and fulfill your inner self's need to create. They can uncover and nurture talents you did not know you had. Who knows, you may even become the next Frida Kahlo in the process!

Expand Your Education

If you are truly interested in gaining knowledge, you will never find yourself with a shortage of things to learn. You can study for both personal growth and general knowledge. Dig deeper into subjects that interest you for either your own benefit or even to upgrade your professional status. Your brain—and your body—will thank you for it.

Go to a Movie

Sometimes your body is wound so tightly that the only cure is to take it somewhere where it doesn't have to think or move. Choose movies that will soothe, entertain, and inspire you.

Minimize Stress

To reduce stress, practice the relaxation techniques discussed previously. Eat healthy foods, exercise your body and mind, and have more fun in your life. If your life is full of stress, decide what changes you need to make and put them into motion. It is not healthy to be beaten down by stress. Love yourself enough to take the best care of your physical and mental being.

Nourish Your Body

While it is good to love your body just as it is, it is also wise to nourish and protect it so that you are able to enjoy a long and healthy life to its fullest. Being *Size Sexy* is not about approving overeating; it's about acceptance of your body and having a positive attitude. A healthy *Size Sexy* woman makes food choices that nourish her body and help her radiate health and beauty.

The first key to healthy food choices is making sure that you meet all of your daily nutritional needs by eating foods from the five major food groups that focus on variety, balance, and moderation. The food groups in the pyramid include the following:

1. Grains
2. Vegetables

3. Fruits
4. Milk
5. Meat and beans
6. Oils

If you eat the recommended portions of these foods daily, you will be well on your way to being a healthy *Size Sexy* woman! Now, let's discuss other ways you can improve your overall health.

Make Healthy Food Choices

Here's reality: Some foods are very good for your body; some are not. Foods that are exceptionally good for you and that you should definitely include in your daily choices include:

- Omega-3 fatty acids found in fish, flax oil, nuts, and spinach
- Colorful vegetables that are rich in antioxidants
- Brown rice, whole-grain bread and pasta, and beans
- Lean protein, fish, soy, and legumes

Foods that have an adverse effect on your health and should only be eaten in moderation include:

- Excess saturated fat (meat, cheese, and fried food)
- Trans fat (margarines, baked goods, chips, and fast food)
- High-calorie food
- Refined carbohydrates like white rice, white bread, chips, pasta, and cookies

Eat Super-foods

No matter what size you are here are some foods that offer incredible nutrition and many other positive benefits.

These foods include:

- Sweet potatoes
- Avocados
- Nuts
- Broccoli
- Salmon
- Dark leafy greens
- Sardines
- Beets

Check with a nutritionist or read nutrition publications to learn more about super-foods and how they can help keep you healthy.

Eat More Fruits and Vegetables

Adding fruits and vegetables to your diet is a great way to nourish your body with vitamins and minerals and to increase your fiber intake. Eating fruit is definitely better for you than eating candy, and it can help you feel good by stemming those dangerous cravings for sweets.

stella's secrets

Your size and weight should not be an obstacle to succeeding in your life and in your career. You can be phenomenal at what you do, and don't let anyone tell you differently.

Eat Breakfast

There was a reason our mothers hounded us to eat breakfast; it really is the most important meal of the day. Our bodies need a healthy breakfast to supply nutrients that were depleted while we slept, and eating a healthy breakfast also fires up your energy so you can start your day feeling good. It is best to eat a light, healthy breakfast, instead of a heavy one—those usually make me feel sluggish and it can be tempting to crawl back into bed. I leave those large—but healthy—breakfasts for weekends or special days when I have more time to enjoy them.

Here are a few healthy suggestions for your morning meal:

- Cold cereal with fruit, nuts, and low-fat milk
- Eggs (any style) with vegetables
- Yogurt and honey with fruit and granola or cereal
- Fruit salad and yogurt
- Hot oatmeal with raisins or berries

*fabulous*quotes

"I never worry about diets. The only carats that interest me are the number you get in a diamond."
—Mae West

Avoid Crash Diets

If you decide—for your own personal reasons—that you would like to reduce your weight, please be sure to stay clear of crash diets. What is a crash diet? Well, it's a diet that is severely restrictive in food choices or that encourages you to eat less than 1,000 calories a day. These diets can be disastrous for your health.

Here are four ways in which crash diets can be harmful to your body:

1. Your body goes into survival mode—holding onto rather than releasing fat.
2. The foods you do eat will not meet your daily nutritional needs.
3. You will lose muscle, not fat, and you need muscles to burn fat.
4. You will likely become a rebound dieter, one who gains back more than she lost.

If you need to lose some weight, eating a balanced, healthy diet is the only truly effective way to lose weight and remain healthy over the long run. It is that simple.

fabulous quotes

"The biggest seller is cook books and the second is diet books—how not to eat what you just learned how to cook."
—Andy Rooney

Recognize Proper Proportions

The world really has gone overboard when it comes to the amount of food they serve in restaurants. Sometimes you will be served two or three times the amount of food that you need—or should eat. You don't need to finish those huge portions in order to enjoy the taste of foods. Take a good example from the French. They eat good, rich, and delicious food but in small portions.

let me tell you!

I keep trying to lose weight but . . . it keeps finding me.

Eat Healthier Snacks

Before you reach for a candy bar or chocolate or a brownie, consider a low-fat piece of cheese with a few whole-wheat crackers, or a cup of yogurt with strawberries or a few tablespoons of granola, or a healthy granola bar. These healthier snacks will stave off hunger and save you hundreds of empty calories—and when you pamper your body by feeding it healthy food, you will feel better about yourself and your choices.

Recognize Food as a Nutrient, Not a Pacifier

Food can be incredibly enjoyable, but don't forget that its main purpose is to nourish your body and provide energy to lead an active life. If you are too focused on eating, you are neglecting the joy of living. Stop using food to soothe a lack of excitement, and get out in the world and whip up your own excitement. Many of us have learned to use food to comfort ourselves, when what we actually need to do is fix the things that are making us uncomfortable.

Eating food *is* enjoyable—and I want you to enjoy everything you eat—but living life is more important than what, or how much, you're eating. Here's another simple fact: If you choose to eat healthy foods that truly nourish your body, you'll live longer and healthier. If you overeat, you will gain weight uncontrollably—and that is not what being *Size Sexy* is all about. So focus on becoming more fit and make an effort to schedule fun activities.

stella's secrets

Just because you have a tendency to gain weight, or because you have accepted yourself as *Size Sexy*, does not mean you should let yourself go and eat uncontrollably. When I find myself craving food for comfort, I try to make good choices, steer clear of junk food, and select figure-friendly comfort foods instead. Instead of potato chips, I'll microwave a sweet potato. Instead of ice cream, I'll have a low-fat frozen yogurt. Instead of a candy bar, I'll have a small piece of dark chocolate. Not to worry, though; when it is time to indulge, I most definitely do!

Exercise Your Body

You better work it, girl! Becoming more positive and bolstering your self-confidence is mostly a mental project, but never underestimate the power of your physical being in creating the overall image you want to project. And by that, I'm not talking about your weight; I'm talking about how good you feel, physically, from the time you wake up in the morning to the time you go to bed.

Exercise isn't simply for weight loss or weight maintenance. It's about feeling your best every day. Exercise also does not mean going to the gym and hating it. There are many ways to be active and have fun at the same time. Part of being in touch with yourself is being in touch with your body, as I mentioned earlier, and there's no more important way to get in touch with your physicality than exercising.

Regular physical activity has many beneficial effects. Here are some of the reasons a *Size Sexy* woman needs—and will soon want—to move her body:

- It helps keep your metabolism functioning at maximum capacity.
- It keeps your muscles toned and strong.
- It maintains bone strength and density.
- It improves and maintains heart and lung function.
- It builds stamina and improves flexibility.
- It boosts your immune system.
- It reduces your risk of cancer.
- It improves your reflexes.
- It lowers stress.
- It benefits your mental health.
- It makes sex more fun.

And if you don't believe exercise can be enjoyable, check out some of these exercise activities that are more fun than work, but still very effective in helping you to get your body moving!

Exercise for Thirty Minutes a Day

Moderate exercise, done for as little as thirty minutes a day minimum, is an amazing way to keep fit and energized, and it can also help you sleep better at night. Don't think of this as a chore; think of it as the least you can do to help your body be healthy and happy. If thirty minutes seems too daunting, break up your spurts of activity into three ten-minute sessions—walk briskly, take a bike ride, or a go for a quick run with your dog around the block. Three bursts of ten minutes each day will meet your thirty-minute-a-day goal. Ideally, you'll also be doing more intensive activities (ones that will make your heart beat faster) each week to stay fit.

Go for a Walk . . . Often

Walking is a fabulous exercise for *Size Sexy* women. Not only does it get you out into the world, strutting your sexy self about, but walking is also a marvelous way to improve coordination and balance, as well as to stimulate bone growth and density, and to build muscular strength and endurance in your legs and the muscles of the back and abdomen that keep your trunk erect.

Plus, you can walk nearly anywhere: in the city, in the country, in a neighborhood, in a shopping mall, or for transportation—and you can do it solo or with dogs or friends or lovers. Walking can be very romantic, so get out there ladies and take a stroll with someone you love!

let me tell you!

Exercise produces endorphins, natural morphine-like hormones that produce a sense of well-being and reduce stress levels. The effect of endorphins can last for hours or even a few days, but beyond that, you have to reproduce them. In other words, exercise makes you feel fantastic. Get some!

Join a Pilates Class

Pilates is a series of gentle exercises done to increase core strength, flexibility, and movement. It works by using the resistance of the body to condition and correct itself, with the goal of lengthening and aligning the spine. Like yoga, Pilates offers a low-impact form of strengthening and toning muscles and also helps you get more in tune with your body. The more you practice Pilates, the more it increases your core strength and your flexibility—and the more it helps you achieve a longer, leaner physique. A smart *Size Sexy* woman will appreciate the benefits of using her body to make her body even more curvaceous and attractive.

Check your area gyms for classes specifically aimed at us *Size Sexy* women, or try workout DVDs aimed specifically at full-figured women.

Practice Yoga

Yoga is another great way for *Size Sexy* women to build additional strength and flexibility without overstressing their muscles, which many aerobic exercises tend to do. Who wants all that bouncing and jiggling that comes with aerobics when the type of stretching one does in yoga brings everything back into balance and helps your muscles stay soft and supple so they can do their job. Since muscles help maintain posture and balance, helping them maintain pliability and strength will boost your overall health, your posture, and your muscles' ability to burn fat. Yoga is a low-impact way to move your body and improve your body. Try it!

Again, check your area gyms for yoga classes specifically aimed at us *Size Sexy* women, or try workout DVDs aimed specifically at full-figured women.

stella's secrets

Don't be afraid to try something new, like antigravity yoga, for example. It offers all the benefits of yoga, but with a lot less strain on your joints and back. This fun, trendy exercise uses a flowing fabric hammock to work your body, decompress your back, and help align your entire body. Check your local yoga centers and gyms for classes and give it a whirl.

Climb Some Stairs

Climbing stairs gets your heart pumping and works your butt and leg muscles, helping them, like no other exercise can, to become sleek and fit. Start slowly and work up to climbing stairs at a brisk pace for ten minutes a day. You'll strengthen your legs, and you'll notice that it will help you keep your heart pumping long after you stop going up the stairs (going down is good, too, by the way).

let me tell you!

If you haven't exercised in a while, always talk to your doctor or get a physical exam before starting any type of stamina-building exercise—just to be on the safe side.

Dance Your Heart Out

Even if you have two left feet, turn on your favorite tunes and let the beat inspire you to move your body. Whether it's in your living room or a local club or studio, dancing is wonderful exercise—and you can be good at it no matter what your size or shape. Don't worry about how you look or whether you are doing the steps correctly. Dancing is good for your body and your soul. Dance your *Size Sexy* heart out and have fun!

If you're game for more social dancing, find dance classes in your area and get in the habit of going often. Another idea is to grab your girlfriends, go out to a club, and start shaking that sexy ass. Not only will your body be happy—because dancing strengthens your heart and your muscle groups, and heightens flexibility—but you might actually meet like-minded men and women you would enjoy getting to know better. And we haven't even mentioned how much fun dancing can be, which should inspire you to want to dance more often.

There are many different styles of dancing, so pick one that appeals to you and get on the dance floor. (You never know: You might just meet your future sexy prince.)

Spend a Week at a Health Spa

For many of us, the word *spa* used to conjure up images of weight loss through deprivation and grueling workouts, but now spas have expanded their consciousness. Today, many spas focus more on overall fitness, health, and relaxation, and offer more attractive, balanced meals and luxury treatments, such as hot-stone massages and mud baths to pamper your body and spirit. Yes, they also encourage you to hike or swim, or try Pilates, yoga, and meditation; you can find these activities in marvelous settings, such as California, Arizona, or Europe.

stella's secrets

The more variety in your exercise routine, the more likely it is that your body will increase its strength, endurance, and flexibility—and the less likely it is that you'll grow tired of your routine. Ideally, exercise should strengthen muscles, benefit the heart and lungs, and build endurance. Find various ways to achieve these goals just so you can be a healthier *Size Sexy* woman—and have fun with it!

Make It Fun

Whatever way you choose to work out, make it fun. Instead of viewing exercise as a chore you have to schedule into your day, view it as a marvelous opportunity to rev up your engine, improve your flexibility and femininity, and have fun!

Spice It Up

If you want to spice up your physical activity, you might want to try these rather sensual activities:

- *Striptease or pole-dancing:* Either one of these activities offers a great workout and will limber up your sexuality. Both will teach you new ways to move your body naturally, unapologetically, and freely. In other words, it's perfect for the *Size Sexy* woman, and it will help you stay in touch with your body and your sexual desires, feel good about your body, and help you master your new sexy moves!
- *Belly dancing:* This is a very sensual and feminine dance. In addition to being good exercise, belly dancing is exotic and vibrant and it will definitely connect you to your sensuality and flexibility by teaching you how to be seductive and erotic in a graceful way. It will also help you connect yourself to those feminine moves—the ones that will make it easy for you to walk that walk and attract admirers.

let me tell you!

Swimming is a great way to move your body. It not only provides an excellent upper-body workout, but it is low-impact and provides a therapeutic effect on all your muscle groups.

Be True to Yourself

Learning to believe that you're beautiful can only happen if you believe you're at your true size, the size your body is meant to be. Beauty is a learned acceptance and the cultural norm of beauty changes over time. Remember, at the start of the twentieth century, the leading sex symbol was Lillian Russell, and in the 1950s, it was Marilyn Monroe. Both of those women would be considered overweight today, yet they were, and still are today, considered sex symbols.

What is really beautiful and sexy is finding what size you are comfortable at and becoming a stylish woman at that size. That is what makes you a *Size Sexy* woman!

So, now that you know how to treasure your body, let's move on to figuring out your figure—which type best defines you and how you can make the most of it.

chapter **six**

celebrate your body: know your curves and flaunt your assets

The idea of this book is to try to help you find your beauty, inside and out, and to inspire every *Size Sexy* woman to find her self-confidence and her personal style. It's time to release the *Size Sexy* woman inside of you, so come on, full-figured goddesses—show them that you rule, and that you can become a fabulous, stylish creature!

Stop Hiding Your Fabulous *Size Sexy* Body

If there is one mistake that is most common among curvaceous woman, it's that many hide their bodies by wearing clothing that is too big. Many women do this because they think larger, looser clothing hides their body flaws, but, in fact, oversized clothing isn't complementary to anyone's figure and often makes people look even bigger than they are.

I hope that after reading the tips in this book, those *Size Sexy* women who wear baggy clothes will find the confidence to accept and accentuate the most beautiful parts of their bodies so they can start feeling attractive and desirable. Trust me, ladies, when you start feeling this way, you'll have a newfound passion and joy to shop for clothes, to get dressed every morning, and to truly have fun with fashion, because that's really what it's all about.

fabulous quotes

"A beautiful woman is someone who pays a lot of attention to herself and knows what suits her."
—Vivienne Westwood, Designer

Many women, not just full-figured woman, also often make the mistake of wearing the wrong clothes on the wrong body. They sometimes blindly follow trends, assuming that if a major designer, or a major clothing chain, has a certain look in the stores, that's the look we should all be wearing. No! If you have the correct shape, and it fits with the trend, by all means, go for it! But you must choose your pieces because they suit *your* body; you have to wear things that are flattering and sexy specifically to your shape. Those belly-baring shirts that were all the rage a couple of years ago are a perfect example among recent fashion trends. You know what I mean, the tight shirts that left many women with their stomachs hanging out everywhere. Honestly, they didn't look flattering on everyone, and I'm not just talking about *Size Sexy* women. Not all so-called skinny women look good in all types of clothing, either. Another disastrous "fashion trend" was the low-rise wave. "Disaster" is the only word I can think of to describe a woman wearing these low-rise pants who shows her behind every time she tries to bend over or sit down. Not that anyone should tell you what you can and can't wear—you should wear whatever you want—but if you want to see a stylish woman when you look in the mirror, and if you want to look inviting and well put together, you have to pay attention to the shape of your body and wear the right fabrics for your shape. Don't wear anything that's too tight, or anything that's too loose. Find the right proportions, the right fabrics, and the right measurements to make sure the clothes you wear complement and accentuate the body you have.

Go Figure: What's Your Body Type?

Of course, everyone wishes they had the classic, curvaceous hourglass figure, but, in reality, women come in all shapes and sizes. Your body type is determined by your genetics, by your bone and muscular structure. Your bones determine where you will be wide and where you will be narrow, and no amount of exercising can change your bone structure. What you can control is how much weight you carry, as women's shapes are formed when weight settles in certain places. When we are young, we tend to gain weight in our hips and thighs, but as we age, many women go from a pear shape to an apple shape, which means much of their weight is now settling in the abdominal area. But remember, there is no one shape that is better than another.

let me tell you!

It is time that full-figured women rule!

A lot of full-figured women make the mistake of not showcasing the most wonderful parts of their bodies by not dressing to highlight those body parts. Whether you haven't yet accepted and embraced your voluptuousness or whether you simply haven't discerned which parts you should be showing off, one way to get in touch with your body and understand which fashions will look good on you is to figure out which basic body type you are. Body types are determined by the width of your shoulders and hips and the girth of your waist. You may want to measure yours so you can definitely identify your body shape and so you can know what your true dress size is as well. Don't shy away from these numbers, as they do not define who you are—only what size you need to buy.

Also, be aware that clothing manufacturers often create their own size structure. But, in general, misses' sizes range from 0 to 20 and women's sizes usually start at 14W. Women's sizes are usually cut more generously than misses' sizes; and 1X, 2X, and 3X sizes typically range from 14W to 16W, 18W to 20W, and 20W to 24W, respectively.

let me tell you!

To dress well, you first have to understand your body's curves and shape—and then learn what looks most flattering on yours.

Most of us *Size Sexy* women will fall into one of the following categories:

- Apple
- Pear
- Spoon
- Bell
- Brick
- Triangle
- Hourglass

To determine your body shape, remove your clothing and stand in front of a full-length mirror. What you are studying is the way your body is proportioned. Do you have a very large bust, a narrow waist, and narrow hips? You are likely an inverted triangle. Do you have a slender upper torso and wide hips and thighs? You are likely a pear. Do you have a rounded shape with an undefined waist, with relatively slender legs and arms? You are likely an apple. Do you have a large, curvaceous bosom and wide, curvy hips with a narrow waist? You are likely an hourglass. Does your entire torso have a thick, almost straight up-and-down rectangular shape? You are likely a brick. These are a few of the most classic shapes, but there are variations with each, such as a bell shape that is a pear with a thicker waist or a spoon that is an inverted triangle with more equally proportioned waist and hips.

It's important to note that no one body shape is better than any other, at least as far as looks are concerned. Knowing your body shape is a tool to help you select a wardrobe that flatters your assets and minimizes the areas that aren't as slim and trim.

Are You an Apple?

The apple body type is usually a rounded shape, with a rounded bust, an undefined waist, and a wider hip at the higher part of the hip. Apples tend to gain weight in their abdomens, particularly as they age or become more sedentary. They may have slimmer necks, arms, and legs, but are mostly identifiable by their round waistline. Oscar-winning actress Kathy Bates is an example of an apple shape.

stella's secrets

I like to see women follow fashion trends. You should always aspire to be fashionable and trendy—but you need to make sure that what you're wearing is flattering to your body shape. Just because you are *Size Sexy* does not mean that you should not look trendy and current!

The fashion ideal for the apple-shaped body is to take the focus away from the fullness or roundness of the upper torso and redirect the attention to the face, hips, and legs, to create an elongated vertical line and balance the upper body with the lower body. Apple-shaped body types also usually have a large face and slim arms and slim legs, which are assets they can bank on when selecting clothing. Basically, if you have an apple-shaped body type you want to try to create a long and lean silhouette.

SOME IDEAS FOR APPLE LADIES:

- Draw the eyes up to your neck, face, and shoulders by wearing voile (or another light fabric) or blouses with small ruffles around the neckline or down the front. Go easy on the frills, however, as you don't want to add bulk.
- Select V-neck sweaters, blouses, or T-shirts with decorative trim around the neckline.

- Wear a pretty scarf over jackets or sweaters.
- If you have a full bust as well, avoid turtlenecks, unless you are long-waisted and have a long, lean neck.
- Focus on your slender legs by wearing tailored, flat-front pants (with no side pockets) that give you a long, lean line.
- Wear tailored pants with wide legs to de-emphasize your midsection.
- Wear dark-colored blouses or sweaters with stream-lined, matching colored pants, and top them with a slenderizing long sweater or jacket in a contrasting color or small pattern.
- If you have great legs, wear shorter skirts or dresses with tights and sexy boots.
- If your hips are on the narrow side, pencil skirts and other fitted skirts will be flattering.
- Empire dresses can work very well as long as they flare out slightly just below your bust line and skim over your midsection.
- Focus on creating an attractive (and sexy) décolletage with a great pushup bra.
- If you have great shoulders, wear off-the-shoulder blouses for nighttime occasions.

WHAT TO AVOID:

- *Wrap dresses.* Unless they skim over your curves, wrap dresses usually bring too much attention to your waistline.
- *Pleated or gathered pants or skirts.* You don't want to add any bulk around your waist.
- *Form-fitting clothing.* Avoid tight garments or anything that clings around your midsection. Choose clothing that glides over your problem areas.
- *Super-baggy blouses or dresses.* Wearing oversized blouses or dresses will make you appear bigger, not smaller. It's okay to wear loose-fitting garments if they're tailored or streamlined, but don't think hiding your frame under a tent will be a flattering look.
- *Belts.* It's very difficult to create a waist with belts on a rounded body because it makes you appear very bulky and square.

Are You a Pear?

The pear body type usually consists of a smaller upper body and a larger bottom, which makes women with this body type appear to have larger hips and thighs, though often with a slimmer waist and a slim neck and shoulder area. Oprah Winfrey is the perfect example of a pear shape. She often looks very slim when photographed from the waist up, even when she is at her heaviest.

The easiest way for pears to look fabulous is to draw attention to their slender upper body and waist. Often, pears will have ample, yet not overbearing, busts, which they can highlight to draw attention upwards from their larger bottom. As with most body types, it's important for pear-shaped women to avoid ill-fitting clothing. Clothes that are too tight or too loose, particularly shirts, can serve to make the bottom look even more disproportionately large.

SOME IDEAS FOR PEARS:

- Draw attention to your lovely neck and shoulders by wearing blouses and dresses with special details like stones, embroidery, and ties.
- If you have an ample, yet not disproportionately large, bosom, softly ruffled blouses can be very flattering and will balance your hips and thighs.
- Choose wide-legged pants with minimal bulk that skim over your hips and thighs.
- Choose skirts that flow over your hips and thighs, or those with narrow waists that flare slightly, which will slenderize.
- Show off your trim waist with fitted jackets, tailored shirts, and belts to cinch your shirts and jackets.
- You have the perfect figure to wear form-fitting sweater sets that you can button or cinch at the waist with a belt or a ribbon.
- If you need to balance your upper body with your lower body, wear square-necked sweaters or blouses with cap sleeves to broaden your upper body.
- Choose accessories like shoulder pads, beautiful pashmina shawls, or scarves, which will all draw the eye to your neck, shoulders, and upper torso.

WHAT TO AVOID:

- *Leggings.* Wearing tight-fitting leggings or skinny pants will only emphasize your hips and thighs.
- *Shapeless dresses.* Wearing loose-fitting dresses will hide your glorious assets—your slender, shapely upper torso and waist.
- *Full skirts.* If they have stitched-down pleats or pleats that begin three to four inches below your waist, they may flatter your figure, but steer clear of full skirts that have the potential to make your bottom look bigger.

fabulous quotes

"Beauty is the sole ambition, the exclusive goal of taste."
—Charles Beaudelaire

Are You a Spoon?

Spoon-figured women are pears whose hips are slender at the top and then widen considerably. If you're a spoon, you may also have a rounder abdomen, but more slender thighs than many pear shapes. Spoons should follow the same guidelines as pears, but you should also take advantage of their thin legs and show them off often. It is also good to balance a spoon shape by wearing blouses and jackets that draw the eye up and don't bring attention to the hips. Buying dresses that fit may prove difficult, so find ones that flatter your lower torso and then find a tailor to size the upper torso. Wearing long, flowy jackets and sweaters, as long as they are lightweight, will help slenderize your hips.

Are You a Bell?

Bells are also very similar to pears, except bells tend to carry a little more weight around their waist and upper hip area. If you are a bell shape, you will want to draw tips from both the apple and the pear, selecting those ideas that prove most flattering to your shape. Empire waist dresses and tops would work well for bells, while anything that draws attention to the waist may not.

Are You a Brick?

The rectangle body type usually consists of a body that is described as "straight up and down." Often these are women who had "tomboy" shapes as young girls—a flat bust and narrow hips. As bricks mature, and particularly as they experience menopause, they will gain weight in the torso, but not in a rounded way like apples or pears. Bricks may have curves, but they won't usually be naturally defined. No worries, though, as there are plenty of tips and tricks to define the curves you do have or to help you give the illusion of curves. More good news: When you gain or lose weight, it is more likely to be distributed or lost proportionately. Also, many women with a brick shape have trim arms and legs that they can use to their best advantage.

The easiest way for bricks to look sexy is to select high-quality, fluid fabrics that reinforce a soft, vertical edge to the boxy shape or that break up the boxy shape.

SOME IDEAS FOR BRICKS:

- Wear wrap tops, scoop necks, and spaghetti straps, which will show off the great upper proportions of your rectangle-shaped body type.
- Don't be afraid to buy padded bras. They can boost what you do have, add curves when you wear form-fitting tops, and even create a sexy décolletage.
- Low-cut blouses and sweaters can be very flattering. Go as low as you dare at night, while being a bit more modest for the office.
- Skirts or dresses in soft fabrics can feminize a boxy shape.
- Pleated or gathered skirts can be flattering, particularly if the pleats are stitched at the top and flare out at the hip.

- If you have slender legs, skinny pants paired with soft, flowing tunic tops can be super-sexy and flattering.
- If you have great arms and legs, show them off! Sleeveless and strapless shirts and dresses and short skirts should be key pieces in the wardrobe of the rectangle-shaped *Size Sexy* woman!

WHAT TO AVOID:

- Avoid boxy jackets, as they only serve to make you look, well, even more boxy. Instead, select jackets that are cut down to the waist, which helps create the illusion of curves in that area.
- Shapeless dresses will just hang on your figure. Choose loose-fitting dresses with darts that narrow the waist.

Are You a Triangle?

Those with triangle shapes can be either a regular triangle or an inverted triangle. *Regular triangles* have very narrow shoulders, a small bust line, and a narrow waist. Their weight mostly settles in their hips, and they will often have relatively thin legs and arms. Basically the same principles that apply to pears will work for regular triangles. If you have this shape, you should wear light shoulder pads to widen your shoulders and balance your hips. Wearing lighter colored tops and tops with decorative details such as ruffles or wide collars, will also help to balance your figure. You can widen your shoulders by wearing square-necked or boat-necked blouses or jacket with epaulets or wide lapels.

Inverted triangles are quite different from their regular triangle counterparts. They have wide shoulders and a large bust line, with a narrow waist and hips. They may also have thin legs and arms. Sherri Shepherd of *The View* is an inverted triangle. If this is your shape, your biggest challenge is to balance your large upper torso with your narrow lower torso. To do this, you will want to adhere to advice that usually applies to women with very full busts. You should avoid turtlenecks or any blouses that do not have a V-neck, and you will also want to wear wide-legged pants and flared skirts to balance your heavier upper torso. It is extremely important for inverted triangles to buy support bras that will balance their figure and make all clothes look better. You can also select blouses and jackets in darker colors and skirts or pants in lighter colors, which will help balance your figure.

stella's secrets

I make up my own mind how I feel about my body and don't listen to what anyone else has to say. I don't know about you, but I've had enough of worrying about what people have to say about my big ass. I think it's a fine ass, and that is all that counts!

Are You an Hourglass?

The hourglass body type projects the ultimate overall curvy shape. In almost everyone's opinion, the hourglass shape is the queen of body types, with hips and shoulders that are nearly the same width, even in profile, which are made even more fabulous by the fact that they are paired with a trim waistline. Lucky girls indeed! If you have an hourglass body type, it's likely that your waist is well defined, your neck and shoulders are probably in proportion to the rest of your body, and you may have slightly larger arms. You are definitely the most sensual, curvaceous diva of all the body types. In short, the hourglass body shape is the utmost in a classically sexy body. Few are so blessed and their numbers include Marilyn Monroe, Sophia Loren, and yours truly—yes, I am a lucky woman (although I consider myself to be an hourglass and a half!).

The most fabulous thing about the hourglass figure is that you don't need many tips or tricks when choosing your clothing—the hourglass figure doesn't need to be hidden, it should only be showcased! You can wear tailored dresses, wrap dresses, and blouses in soft and flowy fabrics, and sophisticated cuts. You'll also look fabulous in clothing that accentuates the waist, such as corset tops and corset dresses in a sturdy fabric such as taffeta. Just remember to play up your assets by choosing clothing that emphasizes those curves and draws attention to your proportionate waist. Even if you are a very full-figured woman, you will look fabulous in dresses that visually cinch in the waist.

Is there anything that hourglass-shaped women should avoid? Of course, no body type is absolutely perfect. You should avoid boxy-shaped anything, overly flowy skirts, and big, loose-fitting shirts . . . unless you want to hide that fabulous, curvy body!

Dress Your Body

Now that we have discussed how to dress each figure, let's take a look at some tips for dressing all full-figured bodies. Basically, it's pretty simple: When in doubt, go basic. Everyone looks great in classic clothing, particularly finely tailored dresses, skirts, slacks, and suits. Unfettered, clean lines, such as sheath dresses, A-line skirts, flat-front pants, and unadorned jackets, flatter a variety of shapes. Plus, as you fill your closet with a wardrobe of classic outfits and learn the fine art of mixing and matching (and accessorizing), you will only need a few new items each season to look updated and fabulous. But no matter what you wear the most important thing is confidence. Confidence will radiate out of you, and will help in your professional, personal, and even your love life.

fabulous quotes

"Elegance is important, courage and dignity essential."
—Diana Vreeland, Former *Vogue* Editor and Legendary Style Icon

A Smooth Silhouette

Build a wardrobe of classic clothing in black, brown, gray, beige, and camel, and you can jazz up classic suits with colorful blouses in lightweight fabrics that add pizzazz rather than bulk.

TO CREATE A CLASSIC SILHOUETTE:

- Wear one-piece dresses that skim over your figure.
- Wear all one color or colors in the same monochromatic tone.
- Choose lightweight jackets or cardigans that flow over your hips.
- Keep jackets or sweaters open rather than buttoned up.
- Add a long, non-bulky scarf to your jacket or sweater.
- Don't wear belts in contrasting colors.
- Wear trouser-length pants.
- Wear longer skirts (proportionate to your height).
- Wear shoes with a one inch or higher heel.

TIPS FOR MAXIMIZING YOUR LONG SILHOUETTE:

- Look for garments that are well constructed and that have darts in strategic places to slenderize your bust, waist, and hips.
- Monochromatic tones slenderize, but they can be dull. To spice them up, use texture to add interest, such as a knit jacket over a silky camisole or a leather vest with jeans.
- If you are petite, avoid large patterns, horizontal stripes, and oversized accessories. Wearing one color will make you look taller, as will wearing long pants rather than crop pants or shorts.
- In winter, wear tights with boots that match your skirt color.
- If you are on the full, full-figured size, avoid wearing large patterns. Opt more often for darker colors, like classic black, navy, brown, or dark gray.
- Don't wear your pants inside your boots unless you have long legs.

Flaunt Your Assets

You always want to take advantage of the best aspects of your figure. If you have sensational wrists and pretty hands, opt for three-quarter sleeves and wear bangle bracelets and watches to show them off. If you have toned, sculpted arms, bare those lovely assets by wearing sexy sleeveless dresses.

OTHER ASSETS AND HOW THEY CAN BE FLAUNTED:

- If you have trim thighs and sexy legs, by all means, wear short skirts, shorts, and high heels. Wear dark-colored leggings with a soft, feminine tunic on top. Be careful, however, if you have slender legs and an apple torso: Steer clear of skinny legs on pants, as they will emphasize your hips and make you look off balance.
- If your bust line is your best asset, wear V-necks that dip sexily southward, or form-fitting clothes that glide over, but do not cling, to your breasts. Classic wrap dresses or tops can be very sexy, particularly when accessorized with a stunning necklace. When choosing necklaces, keep proportion in mind: Too small will make your bust look oversized rather than *Size Sexy*, and too big will compete with your breasts for attention.
- If your booty is your asset, wear skirts and pants that show it off, without overemphasizing it.
- If you have a small waist and trim ribcage, wear sweaters or jackets that you button just under your bust line. Also, wear belts to define your waistline and emphasize those fabulous curves. Avoid empire waists that flare underneath the bust line as they will hide your best asset!
- If your face is your most stunning asset, wear clothing that focuses attention on your face, such as V-neck blouses in flattering colors, with a soft ruffled collar. Add spectacular earrings and necklaces, or wear dramatic hair accessories. Scarves are made for you; buy many in flattering colors and practice ways to wear them.
- If you have fantastic shoulders, wear off-the-shoulder tops and brush your long hair back with a headband to emphasize the bareness of your shoulders.

Disguise Your Challenges

Every *Size Sexy* woman is beautiful, but every body shape has certain challenges. Just as you want to choose clothing that maximizes and flatters your assets, you also want to choose clothing that minimizes or disguises your challenges. Here are a few examples:

- If your upper arms are not taut, you will look best in short sleeves or three-quarter-length sleeves. You can also wear shawls that cover your upper arms or dresses with lace sleeves. If it is really hot, you will actually look better in a sleeveless top than one with small cap sleeves.
- If you have large thighs and legs, stick to pants or long skirts and dresses. Keep proportion in mind, however: If you're short, aim for a long, lean line; if you're tall, you can wear any length. Make sure all your garments glide over your hips and thighs. Wear a body shaper if you are wearing light-colored pants or skirts.
- If your abdomen is your problem area, avoid tight clothing and wear tops that skim over your abdomen. Don't go too loose, as that will have the opposite effect. Soft, fluid jackets in jersey and other flowy fabrics will help you minimize the abdomen area. Avoid belts.
- If you have very large shoulders and breasts, avoid shoulder pads and turtlenecks or blouses that emphasize your bust. Opt instead for V-neck tops and select bottoms that balance your upper torso with your lower torso.

Keep in mind that with the magic of undershapers and the right clothes, you will be able to change your silhouette and create another beautiful body shape.

let me tell you!

What do they say? Sex sells. You know what? They're right. So be the most sexy and seductive *Size Sexy* woman you can be.

Things to Avoid

We will continue to discuss clothing options that will work best for your figure. But in the meantime, you should almost always avoid:

- *Clothing that adds bulk.* Bubble skirts, gathered skirts, or bulky sweaters, particularly heavy cable knits, add unnecessary bulk. If you love nubby textures, try wearing a nubby shawl rather than a jacket or sweater, or a nubby scarf as an accent.
- *Shapeless clothing.* It makes you look bigger rather than smaller. Loosely fitting dresses, blouses, tunics, sweaters, or jackets can work, but the garment should skim your body and highlight any curves.
- *Leggings.* They typically do not work for full-figured women, unless your hips are narrow. If you do wear them, wear long, streamlined tunics to cover your hip area. If you have an apple shape and an inverted triangle shape, opt for wider-legged pants to balance.

let me tell you

I dress sexy for myself first! I am the one who sees and feels it! When my sensuality and femininity show through when I strut my stuff, that is when I feel sexy.

Celebrate Your Body

My whole reason for writing *Size Sexy* is to encourage full-figured women to love their bodies as they are and to celebrate their sexy selves. Begin this journey by embracing your body type and learning to make the best of it. If you are unhappy with the way your clothes fit and you wish to change your shape, the best way is to lose weight—but don't think that you need to lose *all* the extra weight, unless there is a health issue. Never set goals so high that you cannot possibly meet them. Doing so will only serve to make you feel bad about yourself, and you are too fabulous to wallow in low self-esteem. Instead, set a goal to trim down five or ten pounds, just enough to make your clothes glide over your figure and make you look even more beautiful.

stella's secrets

Even I will succumb to low-self-esteem occasionally. There is room for improvement in all of us when it comes to self-image. The key? Feeling good about yourself translates into looking good—when you make the effort to look your best.

It is great to have these beautiful, sexy, voluptuous bodies, so be sure to appreciate yours. Take time often to enjoy the curves you see in the mirror and to compliment yourself by saying, or merely thinking, *I have a fabulous body, I love my curves, I love the softness of my tummy and my breasts, I love my luscious bottom*, and so on. The point is to appreciate what you have and to always be good to yourself—no matter your dress size.

Watch Your Attitude

Remember, you want to project the image of a positive, self-accepting, self-confident woman, and you will achieve that by creating a personal style that meshes with your lifestyle and allows you to be comfortable during each stage of your day, whether you're off to work, to play, to a party, on a trip, or are just hanging out after work. Any time there's an occasion where you have to get dressed up and interact with people, you always want to project the confident *Size Sexy* woman you are.

Sometimes that will mean you have to break a few fashion rules. You always want to be stylish and fashionable according to your lifestyle and according to what really looks good on you. You're going to have to create your personal style, which will likely mean mixing and matching pieces from various designs. The key: Be creative and have fun with it.

So, what should you remember? Well, kept the following tips in mind and you'll be flaunting your *Size Sexy* style in no time!

1. Understand that your body type is determined by genetics. You will probably share the same body type as one of your parents or one of your siblings. You must learn to embrace it.
2. Understand your shape and dress it up accordingly.
3. Accentuate the best—downplay the rest!
4. Accept the fact that what looks good on one body shape, may not look as good on another.
5. You may not be happy with the shape you have, but thanks to style and fashion you can create the visual change that you desire.

Do You Have Style?

So, now that you have some basic information about dressing to flatter your body type, please pay attention to what you wear and how you wear it. Ideally, you want to develop your own style, a manner of dressing that fits your body, flatters your body, and reflects the way you feel about yourself. In the next chapter, we'll go beyond basics to discuss personal style and how you can select clothing and accessories to create the image you want to project. Before we make that leap, please take the following quiz to see where you fit on the style quotient scale:

How do your friends describe your sense of style?

1. They laugh and call me a "fashion disaster."
2. They can see that I try but agree that I never quite get it right—and that I rely way too much on basic black.
3. They think I'm pretty hot. I'm always getting compliments on the way I dress, the outfits I put together, and my jewelry.

When is the last time you organized your closet?

1. There's not much to organize. I don't have that many clothes and mostly wear black pants and skirts. I have skirts and dresses that I've had for eight years.
2. I'll shuffle things around every two years or so, but I rarely throw anything away. I just squeeze new clothes into a space where they seem to fit—like with other conservative blouses.
3. I go through my closet at least every six months. Otherwise, how do I know what I have or what I've grown tired of or what doesn't fit anymore? I like to shake up my wardrobe and the only way to do that is to evaluate what I've already got.

Do you have favorite classics?

1. Do you mean the T-shirt I've had since college?
2. I buy a lot of black and brown, classic colors in classic shapes; and then I throw in white blouses and various sweaters in an array of colors—clothes that always look good that I can mix and match.
3. I have a fabulous denim jacket with classic lines; a fabulous little black sheath dress; one black and one brown suit; a few cashmere sweaters. I love classic shapes and colors, but I like to add a little spice.

How often do you go to a hair stylist?

1. I go to a cheap haircut place and am lucky if I get what I want.
2. I have gone to the same person for at least ten years and we rarely change my hair. It works and I'm used to it this way, although occasionally I get a little bored.
3. I love nothing better than going to have a complete makeover. I'm not a slave to fashion, but I like to experiment and to look updated.

How many pairs of shoes do you own?

1. Eight: Two pairs of sneakers, three black flats, one brown loafer, two casual sandals. Do flip-flops count?
2. Around twelve: I own too many pairs of basic black pumps, but I also have a few fashion colors and kicky styles. I don't include sneakers

and the odd summer sandals as shoes, as they're strictly utilitarian. I do have a few pairs of winter boots.

3. Somewhere between twenty to thirty: I tend to buy classic, expensive shoes that I take immaculate care of. I have classic pumps with varying heel heights in four fashion colors, and maybe three more in black, two in brown, and at least one gray. I also have a small wardrobe of snazzy flats and a few ultra-sexy date shoes—and boots! I also have designer sneakers (fun but not sexy) and high-heeled gladiator sandals (fun and sexy). I stash my special-occasion shoes in containers that slide under my bed.

Answers

Give yourself one point for each 1 choice; two points for each 2 choice; and three points for each 3 choice.

Score: 5 It's a good thing you are reading this book because you need to shake up your closet and your world. Being more aware of and focused on your image will help you find a style that you can call your own—and that will make the impression you secretly desire to make.

Score: 5–10 You've been resting on your laurels. You could look so much more appealing if you would only take the time and effort to learn about fashion and ways to improve your overall image. At least you have got the basics, and that's something we can build on very quickly. Read on.

Score: 10–15 You have some sense of the importance of style and you're making efforts to look your best—which are both excellent indicators that you value your appearance and want to make a good impression. With a little prodding, you can go from a stylish woman to a style maven.

chapter **seven**

create your own style

When it comes to creating a wardrobe with style, a wardrobe that will elevate the way others see you, and the way you see yourself, begin by answering this question: Does your outside—the clothes you wear, the overall impression that your appearance makes—reflect how you feel on the inside? When it comes to dressing up, a lot of how you look on the outside reflects how you feel on the inside. And when it comes right down to it, establishing your personal style really comes down to this one simple idea: You must select fashions that are appealing on *your* fabulously full figure and *your* sexy, sassy shape.

You Are What You Wear

I see a lot of full-figured women who obviously neglect themselves. It's like they have an attitude that says, "It doesn't matter what I wear, because I'm overweight. Who cares? There's nothing I can really do about myself or for myself, so what's the point of getting myself together when I am not happy?"

A lot of full-figured women make this mistake, and they walk around with unstyled hair (maybe it has not been cut for a long time and has long ago lost its shape, or it's too short to match or flatter their body shape); fingernails that are scraggly and bare with ragged cuticles; feet that haven't seen a pedicure in a while, and skin that is dry or clearly not pampered. Unfortunately, I often see women who settled for looking sloppy and even dirty. If there's hair color at all, it's not the proper color, or they're wearing the wrong clothes for their body shape. When you look at someone like that, you think, "Oh, what a slob." And it is clear to all that her failure to tend to her appearance reflects how she feels about herself on the inside.

let me tell you!

They say that clothes speak for you, so make sure you know what yours are saying!

Of course, it isn't always women of size who project themselves this way; there are plenty of skinny women who fall into the same trap. But with full-figured women, most of the time this kind of lack of self-respect is a result of how these women really feel about themselves. They think no one cares how they look, so why should they? Again, it's the inside reflecting itself on the outside.

On the other hand, when you see a *Size Sexy* woman who has it together—she's looking fabulous, she's looking feminine, and she's got it going on—you can tell she takes care of and loves herself. The quality of how she takes care of herself is obvious; she's pleasant to look at and she draws the admiration of others. You can see that she enjoys pampering herself, which is especially pleasing to see in a *Size Sexy* woman, who could have easily thought, "Oh, I'm fat, I'm ugly; no one is going to pay attention so it doesn't matter what I look like." However, this is just not true: People *do* pay attention. You interact with people all the time, and people do take note of how you feel about yourself—and how you reflect your self-esteem in the way you dress. It's important that you remember this. You don't want to be seen as a woman who doesn't respect, admire, or take care of herself.

If you are one of those women whose outside reflects a negative inside, my sincerest hope is that the tips, tricks, and personal experiences I'm sharing with you throughout this book will help you find your positive, self-accepting, beautiful, vivacious, sassy *Size Sexy* self and reflect it back at the world. Remember! You must do this for yourself!

stella's secrets

I know very well that men notice things like grooming. Manicured hands and feet, facial skin . . . these are important elements when it comes to appearing like someone who takes care of herself.

Is Your Personal Style Hiding . . . in Your Closet?

For every woman who seeks to find her personal style and begins the whole revolution of becoming that self-confident, self-accepting, fabulous *Size Sexy* woman we've been talking about throughout this book, it all starts in and from the closet. The first step, then, in pulling together your personal style is to organize your closet, and I don't mean shuffling a few things around to make space or to organize (although that will be an important part of the process). I'm talking about a complete overhaul—a virtual spring-cleaning. So, before you even open the closet doors, be prepared to clean out everything.

let me tell you!

A truly confident woman dresses up for herself first.

Separate the Good from the Bad

The first task, of course, is to go through the clothing piece by piece, pausing to decide which clothing, for instance, you haven't worn for a year or more . . . chances are that if you're not wearing it now you won't wear it again, so get rid of it. I know you think that one day you'll wear it again, but I can tell you from experience that "one day" never comes. You should also pull out clothing that needs repairs or that just doesn't fit anymore. As you review each piece, be truthful with yourself in answering these questions:

- Will I ever take the time to have it repaired?
- Is it a classic or a current piece?
- Is it something I love and would wear if it were repaired or tailored?
- Is it expensive enough to justify having it tailored?
- Will I spend the money to have it tailored?

If the answer is "yes" to all of these questions, then place the items that you designate as "repair and tailor" in a bag. Then, put the bag in your car and take the items for repair or tailoring as soon as possible.

Do you know a good tailor? If not, find one, and fast! We all know that different designers and manufacturers cut the same size differently. Therefore, the same size may fit you differently from one designer to another. But if you have a trusted tailor, you can always have something, anything, made specifically for you. That's what I do; I always create my own designs based on fashions that inspire me but may not be available in my size. A good tailor can also take a garment you love, but which may not fit perfectly, and make it do that very thing!

Be Ruthless

Also, as you clean your closet, be very honest with yourself. Evaluate each item of clothing in terms of its:

- Fashion value
- Quality
- Usefulness
- Whether you love it or not

In order for you to begin your journey to the new you, the self-confident you, you need to start getting rid of the old stuff—clothing that you have outgrown or don't want as part of your new image. Here are the types of criterion you should use when deciding which clothing to keep and which clothing to either toss or give away:

- *Is it cheap?* Cheap clothing rarely projects a fashionable image. Also, cheap clothing tends to fall apart quickly or to look shapeless after you launder it only one or two times. Clothes should be an investment. When in doubt: Invest in quality.
- *Is it out-of-date?* If the style was popular five years ago, unless it is an expensive, classic piece, you should consider letting it go. A fashionable woman does not wear clothing that makes her look dated.
- *Is it flattering?* Even if it is a fabulous piece, if it does not flatter your shape, you must let it go. The whole idea of this makeover is to choose clothing that makes you look your best.
- *Was it a fashion disaster?* We have all bought clothing that lives in our closets for years and is never worn. Often the tags are still dangling from the waistband or collar. Don't delude yourself into thinking you will suddenly wear these clothes. You will not. Give them away and make room for new items.

Once you have sorted through all of your clothing—yes, go through your drawers too!—take those clothes you're unlikely to wear again and give them to somebody else, donate them to the Salvation Army, or just dump them, period. Go through this same process with your shoes, handbags, and accessories. Be ruthless with them, as well. We'll discuss these items toward the end of the chapter, but first you clean out the ones that you know in your heart have to go.

*fabulous*quotes

"I still have my feet on the ground. I just wear better shoes."
—Oprah Winfrey

The only exceptions to your cleanse? A piece that is vintage or classic or is a truly timeless piece. A vintage garment is beautiful and never goes out of style, so you should keep it and cherish it. You can mix it with modern fashions, because again, it will never go out of style. It's a piece with history.

stella's secrets

When in doubt, I ask a friend. Approval for a certain look can come from a good and honest friend who is not afraid to tell you the truth. Find one.

Revamp Your Closet!

We are now going to create a wardrobe that you will be happy to face every day. Start by upgrading your clothing hangers! Get rid of those flimsy wire hangers. Go out and buy yourself a set of wooden hangers—they should all be the same kind and color. Next, organize everything by categories: clothes for work, clothes for special occasions and eveningwear, etc. Then, make up groups of certain articles within each category. By that I mean, clothes for work should have a group of pants, a group of skirts, a group of dresses, and so on. Other categories you might want to consider, depending upon your lifestyle, include: casual daywear, casual evening, casual sporty, workout wear, and beachwear. The most important thing is to make sure that the only clothes in your closet are the ones that make you feel wonderful and confident. And obviously, always keep them clean.

Once you have your closet in order, the next step, and an equally important one, is to have a full-length mirror near your dressing area. I'm surprised by how many women don't own a full-length mirror. But really, how else are you going to know how you look from head to toe when you leave the house every day?

Complete a Wardrobe Assessment

There are a few questions to ask yourself before you start adding new clothes without a plan. Everyone needs to take a wardrobe assessment before creating a fabulous new personal style. Begin by answering the following questions:

1. Which body type am I? Review the various body types we discussed in Chapter 6.
2. Which are my best and favorite body features, the ones I want to highlight?
3. What are my least favorite features, the ones I want to minimize attention to (and don't worry, we all have those, men and women, in all shapes and sizes)?
4. What are my favorite colors?
5. What colors look best on me?
6. Which styles tend to be most flattering on my body shape?
7. Am I prepared to reject certain items that, while they may be trendy, don't necessarily flatter my body shape and curves?
8. Have I considered the kinds of clothing I will need, based on my lifestyle? In other words, do I need more clothing appropriate for my work, my daytime life, my social life, etc.?
9. Am I committed to the idea that when I look good, I feel great?
10. Where do I need to start? What items do I most need to begin fashioning my own personal style?

stella's secrets

I always design and create outfits for myself, because I know *Size Sexy* women shapes very well, and I don't always find things that I like in the stores. So I create my own. Sometimes it makes me feel like creating my own line of clothing . . . hmmmm, maybe someday.

Are You Listening . . . to Your Clothes?

Clothing has a language of its own. And it does send a message that tells people something about who you are and what you do, be it your economic, social, sophistication status, or your moods, whether they are good, bad, or so-so. When I'm not in the best mood, I may want to blend in a little more, de-emphasize my curves, not draw as much attention to myself. But when I'm in a happier mood, that's how I want to dress, in a dressier manner that will show off my fabulous *Size Sexy* self.

Basically, you have to pay attention to what you wear and when: Match yourself and your clothes to the situation you'll be facing that day. And be creative. Every woman should be very creative and imaginative with clothing. Mix vintage with modern, mix designer with nondesigner, mix expensive with nonexpensive—I don't believe in buying an outfit the way it's displayed on the mannequin in a store or the way it's displayed in a magazine. Whether it's designer clothing or not, I believe the most fun part of fashion is putting together the outfits for yourself, mixing and matching. It makes it more interesting, fun, and personal when you mix and match and put together a look for yourself.

fabulous quotes

"Fashion fades, style is eternal."
—Yves Saint Laurent, French Couturier

All those elements come together to create your personal style. Don't be one of those women who obviously went into a department store and bought a pantsuit she saw on the rack. When you create your own style and creatively select your clothes, those who see you will say, "Oh, she really put it together nicely." That's the power of mixing and matching and putting together your own style.

Find Your Inner Fashion Icon

Remember, dressing up is one of the most fun parts of creating a personal look. If you have a problem defining your personal style, you have to consider your lifestyle and your social obligations. And you must come up with an image so appealing to you that you will be inspired to create it for yourself. If you have an image in mind, that's great. If you don't, find yourself a fashion icon or any other kind of icon that might inspire you.

In my case, I love the old-fashioned style of old Hollywood, classic Hollywood, and stars like Shirley MacLaine in *What a Way to Go!,* Rosalind Russell in *Auntie Mame*, Lana Turner in *Imitation of Life*—all of these movies had wonderful, glamorous fashions. Another style icon is Edith Head, an amazing, inspiring woman who created the wardrobes for a lot of those movies; her style is classic. And I also draw inspiration from all the fabulous, strong, and self-confident Hollywood divas like Sophia Loren, Elizabeth Taylor, Marilyn Monroe, and Jane Russell.

fabulous quotes

"Zest is the secret of all beauty. There is no beauty that is attractive without zest."
—Christian Dior

I also love a lot of today's fashion designers, like Jean Paul Gaultier, Thierry Mugler, Balenciaga, Alexander McQueen, Christian Dior, Dolce and Gabbana, and DSquared2, just to name a few. There is a long list of designers I like, but, unfortunately, not that many designers make *Size Sexy* clothes. I wish they did. But it's an inspiration for me. I make my own personal style by combining various fashions together. That's my personal taste, my personal style. You have to try to find your own inspiration, one that is closest to your personality, to who you truly are.

Select an Image to Project

It is very important for you to decide what kind of image you wish to project in your clothing choices. Here's a list of possible images you might want to project. Which one of them most suits your personality, personal tastes, and lifestyle?

- Sophisticated
- Conservative
- Chic
- Classic
- Trendy
- Bohemian
- Sporty
- Glamorous
- All-time sexy
- Or maybe try a mix of a few of the above?

Once you have decided what you want your new image to be, look through fashion magazines or catalogs and tear out pages that feature clothing that fits into your new image. Use the pictures to create a fantasy book of the image you want to make your own. When you go shopping for clothes, take along the book to help you steer clear of making familiar choices and falling away from the new style you want to create. When you are tempted to buy something, see if you could picture it in your new fashion book and if it has the same qualities that you are now choosing. If it doesn't fit into your new look, don't buy it!

You can also do the same with colors and shapes to help you select a wardrobe of clothing, shoes, and accessories that will work well together and that will more clearly reflect the image you desire. Black is good for basic pieces, such as pants, skirts, dresses, and some blouses, jackets, or sweaters, but you also want to add splashes of color that will spice up your wardrobe.

Build a Wardrobe

Now that you have determined your wardrobe needs and your desired image, you are ready to select clothing that will achieve your goals. The first thing to realize is that everyone needs certain items in her wardrobe to create a fashionable image. This is my list of must-haves, basics every closet should have:

The Little Black Dress

Everyone needs a little black dress. I don't think I've ever seen a little black dress—or, in the case of we voluptuous ladies, maybe not so little—that doesn't flatter. It all depends on the cut, and if that cut suits you, that little black dress can go a long way. It can be casual or dressy, appropriate for daytime, late afternoon, dinner with friends . . . just a little black dress with a shawl or a sweater. The little black dress can really take you through a whole day of activities with the right accessories.

Choose a black dress—or two—in a classic shape that flatters your body type. A classic sheath style looks good on most *Size Sexy* women, particularly one that skims over your body and narrows just under the bust and just above the hips to create an hourglass shape. Don't worry about how you feel about your arms. You can always buy a sleeveless sheath and then use shawls, sweaters, and jackets to dress it up or down.

Since this will be a basic in your wardrobe, one that you can wear for many different occasions, make sure that you select a luxurious fabric—one that will always look chic. Just make sure your choice of a dress is feminine and sexy and can be worn for that special moment, day or night.

*fabulous*quotes

"It pains me physically to see a woman victimized, rendered pathetic by fashion."
—Yves Saint Laurent

Courtesy Photography © Guy Sagy

Wear lipstick no matter what. You can get away with skipping all the other makeup, but lipstick is a must. It brings color to your face, and it makes you look finished, but not overdone—that's the best trick I have. The choice of lipstick color is up to you—for me, it's always red.

Courtesy Photography © Ido Izsak

Always say to yourself, "It's great to be me! I am fierce and fabulous, big and beautiful, smart and sexy, feminine and fantastic, curvaceous and confident, sexy and sultry."

Photo by Jean Paul Gaultier

Celebrate your body, know your curves, and flaunt your assets. Don't be afraid to love your body and develop your own distinct, sexy, feminine style to show it off!

I know one thing for sure:

Your perception is *your* reality. Walking into this shoot for *Italian Vogue* (see page 38), I knew I belonged there. Remember that if you view yourself as fabulous at any size, then you will feel fabulous and enjoy your life—no matter how much you weigh at any moment.

Courtesy Photography © Ido Iz

Create your own style. Establishing your personal style really comes down to this one simple idea: You must select fashion that is appealing to your fabulously full figure and your sexy, sassy shape. It's time that full-figured women rule!

Courtesy Photography © Yaki Halperin

If your face is your most stunning asset, wear clothing that focuses attention there. Add spectacular earrings and necklaces, or wear dramatic hair accessories. Scarves are made for you; buy many in flattering colors and practice ways to wear them.

Be sexy.
Strut sexy.
Live sexy.

Think of yourself as a voluptuous glamour goddess and walk around letting others know your secret—that you are all that and more!

Photo by Paolo Roversi

A Few Well-Made Trousers

Every woman needs a few pairs of black and at least one pair of gray and neutral color trousers that she can use to create a basic wardrobe. If you select high-quality trousers, again in a luxurious fabric, they will offer you many opportunities to look your best. And by pairing trousers with mix and match tops, you will be able to create several different looks. Make sure that you are buying a contemporary style, pants that fit properly, and pants that flatter your shape. We discussed body shapes in the previous chapter, but, in general, *Size Sexy* women will want to choose flat-front trousers without pockets on the side and with straight, flared, or wide legs. If you have trouble finding pants that fit or can only find pants that don't fit in the hips or the waist but are perfect in every other way, buy them and take them to your tailor.

A Few Basic Skirts

Like trousers, every woman needs several black skirts, as well as some in beige or gray that will allow her to build a wardrobe of choices. For these choices, stick with knee-length skirts and one or two basic shapes, such as pencil skirts (for those with narrow hips), an A-line shape, or slightly flared skirts. These will be your basics, and then you can add skirts in different colors or shapes for fun. If you want to have a little more fun, you could introduce texture by buying flowy and classy fabrics.

A Black Turtleneck

Every woman needs a black turtleneck. Yes, even if your neck is short and your bosom is large. (You can always lengthen the appearance of your neck by wearing long necklaces or scarves that draw the eye down.) Consider cashmere or another luxurious fabric for your classic sweaters, as they will always make you look fabulous, even when you pair them with jeans.

Two Crisp White Blouses

One also needs at least two crisp white blouses to look fresh and professional. Buy unfettered blouses that you can wear under business jackets and denim jackets, blouses that you can dress up or down. When choosing white blouses, stick with all cotton, as blended fabrics will often yellow quickly or appear limp.

let me tell you!

Getting dressed is not just about current fashion trends. It is about combining your personality, your character, and your personal style.

Two Elegant Blouses

One needs at least two elegant blouses to wear under jackets for work or with a shawl for dinner. Choose blouses that flatter your shape and will lend themselves to accessorizing in a variety of ways, i.e., keep the lines clean and classic. Silk would be a fabulous choice for elegant blouses, and although you may want one ivory and one black, this is also a place where you could choose a fabulous yet neutral color that is in season.

One Classic Black Suit

Just as you need a little black dress, you also need at least one very classic and very classy black suit. Because they can be expensive, make sure that you select a style that will not look dated in a year or two. Also, this is another place to splurge, as you will have many occasions to wear this suit, and those will always be times when you want to look your best.

Complementary Clothing

Other items that every woman will need in her wardrobe include the following basics:

- A few silk or classic sweater sets to pair with the skirts and trousers
- A long black skirt for romantic evenings
- Feminine camisoles to wear under jackets and sweaters
- Additional blouses in colors for work and dressy occasions
- Two pairs of dressy jeans—no sloppy or "mom" jeans
- One wool coat; lightweight if you live in a warm climate
- One trench coat; always make it a classic trench shape
- One leather jacket; black is always good
- One stylish denim jacket, one you can pair with dressy and casual wear
- One fabulous, feminine shawl that you can wear to dinner or on dates

Once you have a classic wardrobe, you can mix and match and add clothing and accessories that will further express your style and reflect your unique personality. Oftentimes it is best to buy your basic wardrobe in neutral colors and then add color in with fashion items.

let me tell you!

Don't Be a Fashion Victim: Don't simply wear what is on display or fashionable at the moment; make sure it suits *your* body and *your* desired style.

Buy the Proper Size

A lot of designers who create beautiful clothes, unfortunately, don't make them in sizes that fit us curvaceous, full-figured women. And that's really too bad, because basically all it takes is a little more fabric to make something for someone who is *Size Sexy* than it would take for someone who is a tall, skinny woman.

Some designers, happily, do create full-figured sizes. But that doesn't necessarily mean the clothes will fit you—be suited to your shape—even if the size seems right. Wearing that trendy piece of clothing is never more important than wearing something flattering that actually looks good on your body. The cut of the clothing means a lot; it determines whether or not a shirt, skirt, or pants will fit and be appropriate for a certain type of body. Something that looks great on a tall, skinny model may fit but not be attractive on a different body type. It's just a fact.

let me tell you!

Dear Designers . . .

I'd love it if you designed more *Size Sexy* clothing and defined your sizes so they are a little truer to a consistent and universal size factor. I'd love it even more if more fabulous couture designers created clothes for the curvaceous and full-figured woman.

Remember, all you have to keep in mind is that the styles you do for the smaller size women could also be whipped up for the *Size Sexy* woman. All it takes is a little more fabric, or maybe a little more time.

But we need more young-looking, stylish designs made with good-quality fabrics. And you have nothing to worry about, because I assure you we *Size Sexy* women will make those clothes look good!

Love, Stella!

Even among full-figured clothing designers and among the range of *Size Sexy* sizes, there are styles that don't always flatter the *Size Sexy* body. I don't understand why plus-size designers don't create more stylish, flattering, and sexy-looking clothes with nice luxurious fabrics. We're all shaped differently, so clothes look and fit differently on each and every one of us. You really have to stick to what looks good on you, what is flattering on *your* body, *your* body shape. Because when you create the look that is really best for your body, that's when you're really going to look and feel good. So be true to yourself and be true to your body when it comes to style and fit and what is appropriate for your personal style. Keep that in mind when you're shopping—it's not worth it to buy something trendy if it doesn't look good.

Accessorize to Glamorize

There is no doubt that accessories can enhance an outfit. They can even bring it back to life. Sometimes you may wear a piece that, by itself, is totally dull, and it doesn't feel like it's alive. Sometimes all it takes is a couple of accessories to make it pop.

stella's secrets

I like big, statement pieces of jewelry. I'm a big girl, and I like big jewelry—otherwise, it disappears. I especially like big earrings and the big cocktail rings—they're my favorite. *Size Sexy* women can really carry those, even better than smaller women.

As with all other areas of fashion, there are some basic rules of thumb to follow when it comes to accessorizing:

- Necklaces, chokers, and other big statement pieces of jewelry are only right on women who have the neck to carry them, meaning they have a nice chest and nice breasts. If you have a small chest, it is difficult to carry a big necklace.
- If your neck is short and your face is big, you definitely don't want to wear a choker or a big, chunky necklace, because that will just make your upper torso look smaller and scrunched together. The accessories will overwhelm that area, and that is not appealing. Accessories should add to your look, not detract from it.

- Chunky beads, draping necklaces, and pendant necklaces can work well on most body types, because they'll help give you an elongated look.
- Bangle bracelets are also flattering on most women and are always in fashion.
- Hoop earrings, to me, are always fashionable, always in style. In different sizes and colors, they can really pull an outfit together.
- Chandelier earrings are a fabulous accessory for a dressy look, and if incorporated properly, can even work with a day look.
- Rings. I live for rings. Rings for me are the ultimate jewels. Not too many, but a nice big chunky one on each hand can be great.

What's Your Bag?

Some of my favorite accessories are also shoes and bags. For that matter, I don't really know any woman who doesn't love shoes and bags. Men don't understand it; when I come home with packages, my husband always asks me, "How many bags do you need? How many shoes do you need?" My answer: an endless amount. Handbags and shoes are a fabulous way to make a fashion statement—to flatter your shape and to express your style and make it sing. Consider them investment dressing and don't be afraid to buy high-quality handbags and shoes in classic shapes and design; they will last a long time and will always give you the look you want. A few of my favorite handbag shapes include:

- *The clutch.* I like clutches in bold colors, metallics, and in various fabrics. I even like clutches that are bejeweled. The clutch is the all-time most perfect bag for the evening.
- *The tote.* It's more casual and perfect for daytime, just like the shopper bag.
- *The messenger bag.* It's the perfect errand bag. It's very practical, because you can walk around and have your hands free. It's also comfortable across your body and there are some really beautiful ones out there.
- *Big bags.* They're great for daytime, depending on you, your personality, and the amount of stuff you like to carry around with you. A big bag can balance a full figure, but be careful not to go too big, especially if it hits you at the widest part of your body.

And Then There Are . . . Shoes!

Many *Size Sexy* women—and women of all shapes and sizes—also seem to buy the wrong shoe for their feet. This, again, stems from the idea that some women assume that whatever footwear is in fashion, or is trendy at any given time, is the footwear that they should be wearing. Wrong, wrong, wrong! This is especially true for women with big feet who try to squeeze that foot into a narrow or pointy, low-cut shoe, only to find that their shoe runneth over. That's not very attractive, and it's certainly not very sexy. We're not looking for a Cinderella story here, ladies. . . . You have to find the shoes that fit and complement your feet, not the other way around.

Basically, once you have a wardrobe of basic shoes—black, brown, beige, and taupe pumps at varying heel heights (including flats), a few pair of dressy boots, and a few divine sandals—you should feel the absolute necessity to buy shoes you love—for whatever reason. High-heeled shoes make a powerful statement, as do sexy stilettos and mules. When you see a shoe that you know will complement your shape and showcase aspects of your personality that you long to feel—and to have others observe—treat yourself! After all, shoes are the perfect way to express your style and make a true and unique fashion statement.

However, there are a few rules that a *Size Sexy* woman should follow when choosing shoes:

- *Shoes should be comfortable.* They have to fit you correctly. If you're not comfortable, it will be very difficult to project your fabulous, confident self to the world, and it makes perfecting your sexy walk almost impossible.
- *Shoes should be versatile.* You need high-quality shoes that will look good when worn with a variety of outfits, for a variety of occasions.
- *Shoes should be tasteful and have to match the outfit and the occasion.* The only time to wear sneakers is for very casual or athletic purposes. Sandals can have two purposes: You can wear them for a very stylish day look or summer casual eveningwear. You should have a pair of jeweled sandals and one metallic.
- *Flip-flops do not make a favorable fashion impression.* Save them for the beach.

- Choose shoes that elongate your legs, such as low-throated pumps or a shoe that does not wrap around the ankle.
- Heels will make you taller and appear trimmer. They are good for every occasion, day or night, and will give you that sexy feminine walk.
- Go for shoes in a light color in summer such as beige, taupe, or white as long as they fit your foot properly.
- Don't buy shoes with tiny "kitten" heels, as they will make you look bigger—and wobbly.
- If you have gorgeous feet, don't worry about any particular style—if they fit, buy them!

Stella's Prescription: Retail Therapy

Shopping is one of the most pleasurable activities for a *Size Sexy* woman who truly appreciates what she's got and who wants to look her very best. And yes, of course I have a few shopping tips to share!

- Avoid shopping on the weekend, but if it's the only time you have available, go early in the morning to avoid the crowds and make your shopping experience as relaxing as it can be.
- Wear something comfortable and easy to remove when you know you will be trying on clothes. In the summer, wear sandals. In the winter, try not to wear boots or sneakers or other things that take a long time to remove and put on again. Shopping should be full of fun; avoid anything that makes it stressful!
- Go shopping when you're in a good mood.
- Take a messenger bag or some other bag that allows you to shop hands-free.
- Don't carry too much stuff in your bag; avoid feeling weighted down while you're shopping.
- When shopping at the mall, leave your coat in the car or check it—remember, hands-free shopping!
- When going into a fitting room, take at least two different sizes of each garment with you, because, as we've all experienced, sizes vary from designer to designer.

- If you're having a hard time making decisions, don't panic. Buy things you think you'll love and take them home to try them on at your leisure, in your lighting, in your mirror, and with the things you already have in your closet. But remember, respect the clothes; if you're going to be making returns, keep them in pristine condition for someone else to enjoy.
- Be relaxed and enjoy your shopping experience!

stella's secrets

Be a resourceful girl. There are many print and online catalogs filled with fabulous *Size Sexy* clothing options. Begin your search by perusing the Appendix, where I list some of the best websites for *Size Sexy* women to find fabulous clothing and accessories. Then, if you haven't found your groove, Google "plus-size clothing" to find even more style resources and shopping websites.

The most important thing is to keep in mind that your shopping trip is going to be different from the experiences you had before reading this book. Now you're going in as the new you, the sexier, self-confident you, with your new style and your new look. So enjoy creating that new look for your new *Size Sexy* self!

So Now You Have *It!*

Before we move on to the next chapter, where we will put the sex in *Size Sexy*, here are a few more things to keep in mind as you go about creating your personal style:

- You don't have to be drop-dead gorgeous and look like a supermodel to be stylish and attractive. And I hope that you don't believe that thin equals beautiful. There are plenty of thin women out there who don't have style and don't know how to dress themselves in a stylish, flattering, confident, and beautiful way.

- With the new *Size Sexy* stylish you, you will find that you may be the first one to be noticed when you walk into a room, and I hope that by now you are ready for it. After reading this book and learning to believe in yourself, you'll be ready to make an entrance. So, put your shoulders back, boobs out, butt perked up, and head held high—make your entrance grand with a fabulous attitude, presence, and grace!
- High heels really do a lot for a woman's appearance. The minute you slip them on, you're all attitude and your body posture changes. You're instantly taller and your legs look sleek and long and smooth. Your femininity is aroused, and the heels will also help accentuate your curves and your voluptuousness. Just make sure you know how to work them by practicing before you hit the pavement.

And all I have to say now is, work it, girl!

Are You Sexually Savvy?

Yes, ladies, in the next chapter, we'll finally discuss sex, a topic that makes some quiver with anticipation and others quiver with embarrassment. But, before we walk through the boudoir together, let's see how you rank on sexual awareness.

Where and how often do you buy your lingerie?

1. Costco, Sam's Club, or Walmart—wherever the best cotton panties can be found at the best price. I buy my bras from Target or Kohl's or whatever store is having a sale when I need new bras, i.e., when my old ones are falling apart.
2. Usually from a department store or from mail-order catalogs. I have a favorite brand of bras and panties that I know really work with my figure, so I always buy the same ones. I buy maybe three bras every year and about twelve new panties every year.
3. Victoria's Secret and upscale department stores mostly. I have a wardrobe of bras and panties that I am always adding to when I see

something particularly sexy or find something that flatters my figure. I believe in updating my lingerie every three months.

What do you wear to bed?

1. When alone, T-shirts with cotton or flannel bottoms, depending on the season. When not alone, cotton camisoles with cotton or flannel bottoms.
2. I buy cotton nightgowns from Marshall's or Target. Some are just utilitarian cotton, but some are very pretty with feminine details. I have two nightgowns for those nights when I have a guest—and they're somewhat sexy, or at least they have a slinky feel.
3. It depends on who's climbing into bed with me! Even when alone, I love to wear pretty nightgowns that make me feel feminine and special. When sharing my bed with a lover, I love to wear sexy but elegant lingerie, something that will please him, make me feel saucy, and will be easy to slip out of.

When is the last time you had a date?

1. I can't remember.
2. It's been at least eight months, since I broke up with my last boyfriend. I just haven't felt the urge to get in the game again. Sometimes it's easier to sit home in sweats, watching television, or to go out with my girlfriends for dinner and a movie. Men aren't knocking down my door. . . .
3. Two weeks ago, and he was a cutie! I love to date, and if I don't have someone asking me out, I ask someone out! Life's too short not to be having fun.

When you do date, how do you dress for a date?

1. If it's a casual date, I would wear jeans; if it's dressy, I would wear whatever I had worn to work that day.
2. If it's someone I am excited about, I wear something very feminine—a skirt or dress—with high heels. It just makes me feel sexier if I dress up a bit and make a little extra effort to look my best.

3. I go all out—I'll take a perfumed bath, wear my hair in a sexy do, and wear something sexy, like a tight pencil skirt or a short mini-skirt. I love to wear clothing that emphasizes my femininity and lets him know that I'm a girl who likes men and that I am very interested in him as a man.

Do you know how to make the most of your physical assets?

1. I mostly do whatever I can to tone down my large breasts and hide those parts of myself that I would be mortified for a man to see.
2. I do like to show cleavage—not too much, just enough. Otherwise I mostly camouflage my problem areas and wear very pretty blouses that bring attention to my face.
3. I love to show off my curves, to wear things that cling where clinging looks sexy and things that glide where attention should not linger. Basically, I know my body very well, what looks sexy on me, and how to strut my sexy self out into the world.

Answers

Give yourself one point for each (1) choice; two points for each (2) choice; and three points for each (3) choice.

Score: 5 You have been sitting on the sidelines so long, you have forgotten how to play the game. Your sex appeal and your libido need a makeover. Repeat after me: "I am a beautiful woman with needs and desires . . . and sex is fun!"

Score: 5–10 Girlfriend, it is time for you to schedule a love life on your calendar. You're doing some things right; you just need a push in the right direction and a little more inspiration. Clean out your lingerie drawers and get ready for a shakeup.

Score: 10–15 You are a love goddess, but I'll wager that we will have a few tips that will escalate your game and bring even more love into your life.

chapter **eight**

find a lover

As I mentioned in Chapter 2, voluptuous and full-figured women have been admired throughout history, going back centuries to when Catherine the Great, a smart, beautiful, full-figured woman, ruled Russia. When Catherine II wasn't serving as the empress of Russia or corresponding with her friend Voltaire, she kept herself busy—*quite* busy in fact—with a string of men, including a husband and many lovers. Catherine's last lover, in fact, was Prince Zubov, who was twenty-two years old when the sixty-something empress invited him into her bed (you go, girl!).

I'm happily married, and my husband Dov loves me and adores me, and adores my shape. He finds me beautiful and sexy. He is an amazing husband and a very special man, and we've been together for sixteen years. We met each other through a mutual friend in New York and got closer when we saw each other again when he was doing hair for fashion shows in Paris—he's a wonderfully talented hair stylist. And it was truly love at first sight.

If you're dating someone right now, good for you! I hope he loves—and lusts after—your *Size Sexy* figure. If you haven't found your dream guy, it's time to invite love into your life. Read on to learn how!

Body Language Is Universal

When it comes to dating and dealing with men and being a woman of confidence, I firmly believe that body language is universal. Whatever self-confidence you feel is expressed by your body language most of the time, by how you carry yourself in the world. Back in my single days, before I met Dov, I never had a problem in that department at all. On the contrary, I dated, I went out, I partied, I danced; I lived life to the fullest as a *Size Sexy* and single woman!

I was always the adventurous type and traveled around the world, exploring other cultures. In each of these countries—France, Greece, Germany, Italy, Israel, Egypt, Morocco, Holland, and Spain—I always had admirers who wanted to spend time with me. No, I did not date all of them, but I enjoyed their company; they took me traveling, to dinners and parties, and enjoyed being with me. They admired me for my confidence, my sensuality, my *joie de vivre*, and my voluptuous body. As for me, I was just having a good time being admired. I loved being a full-figured woman with voluptuous curves—one with so much confidence that men would admire her; I felt free to have a blast.

We are just like animals in the wild that communicate through body language and men have a good sense of feeling what women are transmitting. They read body language very well and that language is universal. The vibe you should be sending is that of a fun woman, someone to be socialized with, someone who is self-confident, sassy, feminine, intelligent, and sexy—outgoing, but not easy to get (catch my drift?).

stella's secrets

I don't waste my time with insecure men. It takes a secure and confident man to love and admire a *Size Sexy* woman without judgment, to see her for who she is and not for what size she is. Don't waste your time with men who don't appreciate you just as you are. Go out and find yourself a secure and confident man who will respect you and enjoy your fabulousness.

What I hope you will understand is that there are men who love and adore full-figured women. And the way you come across all depends on how you represent yourself. So, if you are having a problem in that department, maybe it is time to understand a few things and make some changes in your life. I am sharing these truths in my life in hopes that my experience, philosophy, and attitude toward life as a full-figured woman will help you uplift yourself and become a happier, more confident *Size Sexy* woman.

Bust Negative Myths

While I was doing research for this book, I was genuinely surprised to discover how many people think that full-figured women get a lot less action in the dating field than the average-sized chicks. Why is that? I can reassure you that this was never my experience, but because so many full-figured women fall prey to this idea, let me give you a few examples of why you may feel this way and a few ways you can reverse it. First I will list the common misperceptions, and then I will explain why they are false and how you can change your thinking.

Full-Figured Women Can Never Be Happy

You don't believe that a full-figured woman can be happy? Well, trust me, there are a lot of happy *Size Sexy* women on this planet, and a lot of them have active social lives, work in exciting careers, and enjoy hot and romantic sex lives. If you are not happy, you need to work on self-love and self-acceptance. Begin by not taking criticism so harshly—from others and from yourself. Lighten up on yourself, and then you will see how happy you can be.

Men Don't Desire Full-Figured Women

Why would you have any fear of not being admired or desired by men because of your full-figured size? As I have already noted, there are many men who love curvy, voluptuous *Size Sexy* women. Improve your self-image by upgrading the way you look. Be more feminine and attractive with an attitude to follow by using my beauty tips.

Men Don't Respect Full-Figured Women

You are concerned that men will not treat you with respect? Well, if you treat yourself with respect, then men will respect you back no matter what size or shape you are. If you want respect and demand respect, it will be there for you. Begin by treating yourself with respect: Don't be promiscuous, and have high expectations for what you deserve.

Only Skinny Women Are Sexy

Some say you can only be sexy if you're skinny, and from the number of images we see in fashion magazines and movies and television shows, there may be many who harbor this false belief. Well, let me tell you, honey, do you know how many skinny women there are out there who are not one bit sexy—or even feminine for that matter? You can be sexy at any size; remember, being sexy is a state of mind, not a condition. And if you are in a sexy state of mind, you will spread sensuality and femininity that is full of major sexy attitude with major curves to follow.

It's Not Possible to Change My Image

Do you really think you are incapable of changing your image? In reality, are you are really afraid that you can never improve your self-image? Well, don't worry. You can change both! All you have to do is work to raise your self-esteem and change how you feel about your weight. I want to help you believe that. I want to show you how to find that sexy woman inside yourself, just like I have, and to be that strong, confident, full-figured, big, sexy woman who loves herself and has no problems finding her man.

fabulous quotes

"I think I'll never run out of things to accomplish, as long as I'm alive, because there's so much to learn, and so much to do. I always feel like I have so much further to go, personally, spiritually, emotionally, mentally, and physically."
—Queen Latifah

Love Yourself

Confidence is the ultimate in sexy. There is nothing more attractive, more seductive, than someone who is confident and embraces her life. Confidence is attractive; it is influential. It doesn't matter what size or shape you are, confidence is a very attractive thing at work, in your social life, and at home. No matter whom you come into contact with, confidence and self-acceptance are very, very appealing. They attract people to you, as acquaintances, as friends, as family, as lovers.

Of course, sometimes conjuring up that confidence is easier said than done, and, as with most challenges in life, this is a good place to find yourself a role model. We discussed the importance of role models in Chapter 4, but it's important here too. So, find yourself someone you can look up to, a full-figured woman, a woman of confidence.

If I become your inspiration, it means that I did a good job of connecting to you through my experiences, and my life as a positive, confident, fabulous *Size Sexy* woman. It means I will have achieved something by writing this book, which is exactly why I began this project. I know how many women are struggling and suffering in their everyday lives, struggling with their size, their shapes. I understand that. But I chose a certain path, one that I have shared with you throughout the book, and that path has taken me to some amazing, wonderful places. You can choose a path that will take you somewhere amazing too!

let me tell you!

I speak two languages: femininity and body.

The ways I choose to deal with my size and shape have earned me respect and admiration. Having a very active social life, I never for a split second stood around thinking, “Oh, my ass looks so big” or, “Next to this girl, I look double her size.” Who cares? I feel gorgeous and beautiful and sexy. That’s what you have to project and that’s what will attract people to you.

A Positive Attitude Is Infectious

Being confident not only attracts people in general; it *really* attracts men. Think about it—what man wouldn’t rather be around and with a woman who’s confident in herself, someone with some spunk and attitude, rather than someone who is insecure and doesn’t project any personality? Who *wouldn’t* rather be around that kind of person? So be confident, feisty, and strong-minded. Those are the kind of women that keep men on their toes and most men consider that to be very sexy.

stella’s secrets

I know this about men for certain. Men come to love the one they are sexually attracted to. So, if you want your man to be sexually attracted to you, play up your femininity and walk around feeling sexy. His eyes will follow you, and so will his heart.

Embrace Your Inner (and Outer) Goddess

I always say, think of yourself as a sexy goddess. As we talked about earlier, sexiness in a woman is something that is showcased by your body language: it's walking with grace, swinging your hips, touching and playing with your hair—all those elements make a woman sexy. The power to draw attention to you without saying a word—flirting with the eyes; thinking bodylicious, erotic, luxurious, and glamorous thoughts; and moving gracefully and deliberately—that's what creates a *Size Sexy* package.

All most women want is to be sexy, to feel free to behave in a certain way at a certain time. There are really many different ways that you can portray sexiness. You can be demure sexy, glamorous sexy, mysterious sexy. Part of creating your personal style means finding the version of sexiness that suits you.

let me tell you!

Empower yourself from head to tail and walk around with the attitude of a lion and the beauty of a peacock. When you enter a room, make those heads turn slowly but surely.

Accentuate the Positive

You always have to remember that every woman, whether she's skinny, fat, or in-between, will always have parts of her body that are prettier and more perfect than other parts of her body. No matter what, you have to accept yourself and your proportions. Let's face it: You want to draw attention to all the right places and start feeling good about the best parts of your body. So, what is the most sexy, feminine, fabulous part of your body? How can you showcase that hourglass figure or decadent décolletage to attract the man of your dreams? Use the guidelines that follow to bring attention to your best assets and watch your sexiness skyrocket!

Are You a Boobs Goddess?

Then wear deep, deep—but never cheap!—V-neck and round-neck tops. You must flaunt your décolletage by pushing it up and forward and keeping your posture straight. A plunging neckline will emphasize the fact that you are big and proud, and this is just the start of becoming a confident *Size Sexy* woman! And don't worry if your décolletage is not as ample as you'd like it to be—it's nothing that a good push-up and a few little tricks I'll teach you won't take care of. The most important tip: Wear them proudly.

Are You a Shapely Hourglass Goddess?

If you have a generous bust and hips with a narrow waist, you are an hourglass-shaped figure—though, in a *Size Sexy* case, that means you are actually an hourglass and a half! Be proud if this is your shape, as the small waist makes for the ideal silhouette. And in this case, it's all about cinching, cinching, cinching. That is the beauty of a small waist, showing the curves—and men love those curves. If you don't have that small waist, there are some tricks you could use to enhance it—see Chapter 6.

Are You an Amazonian Goddess?

If you tower over others and have luscious long and healthy legs, then you are made for short, short, short dresses and tight leggings. Don't be shy about showing those legs. Having long legs also makes you the ideal fashionista to wear boots: boots to the knees, above the knee, ankle boots, and even boots to the mid-calf, which a lot of women can't get away with. When shorter women wear them, they can make them look small and boxy. Goddesses with long legs also look fabulous wearing dresses with splits and skirts with splits. A split on the side is a very sexy look for a woman with long legs, as long as, of course, you always keep your legs shaved and luxuriously moisturized.

Are You a Shoulder and Neckline Goddess?

If your best feature is a combination of your bust and neck, then you've got it going on! You can't go wrong with off-the-shoulder blouses, or wearing turtlenecks, chokers, and gorgeous big necklaces. Women with a short neck cannot wear big chokers and big necklaces, because they'll look like they have no neck. But if you have a nice long neck, you have the luxury of accentuating it and decorating it with fabulous statement pieces of jewelry.

Are You a Beautiful Arms Goddess?

If one of your best features is your toned, fabulous arms, you should wear short sleeves, no sleeves, or dresses that are totally strapless. Also, be sure to adorn your wrists with beautiful bracelets that you can easily stack up. You can also wear tighter sleeves to show off those arms. If you are blessed with the combination of a gorgeous neck, breasts, and arms, you've hit the jackpot. Off-shoulder blouses and dresses will look very sexy on you, and you can pull up your hair to show off your neck and draw attention to your face.

let me tell you!

Men love a woman with sexy curves—and attitude.

How to Find Your Sexy Man

Trust me, ladies, there are plenty of men in this world who love and appreciate *Size Sexy* women. Men like curves—it's as simple as that. While fashion magazines, movies, and TV shows seem to prefer thin women, men like a little padding, a soft curve, ample breasts, and booties. They are also very attracted to women who feel sexy and confident, women who take good care of themselves, dress to look their best, and aren't shy about strutting their stuff in the world. I've had many men respond to me—no matter my size—so I'm offering up these tips to help you find the sexy man of your dreams:

Look Good, Smell Good

This advice may sound obvious, and maybe not so important, but trust me, men notice things like hands and feet. Make sure yours are impeccably groomed, and make sure your signature scent will make (and leave) an impression on him. We discussed ways to dress sexy in the last two chapters, and we'll discuss grooming in the next chapter. Take this advice to heart and begin pampering yourself and dressing yourself for success—in the workplace, in your social life, and in your romantic life.

*fabulous*quotes

"Look for the woman in the dress. If there is no woman, there is no dress."
—Coco Chanel

Develop Excellent Posture

Let your body talk. Keep your back straight, shoulders forward, head up, décolletage tastefully showcased; again, never underestimate the importance of body language and great posture! When you stand up straight, it elongates your torso and makes you look taller and more elegant. Also, it helps your clothes look better on you. If you have a tendency to slouch, practice by standing against a doorframe and pressing your shoulders back. This will help your body learn how it feels to have good posture. You can also do as many have done before and practice walking with a book balanced on your head.

Make Him Your Focal Point

Everyone likes to be the center of attention, and men love it when a woman focuses her full attention on whatever he is saying. Look him in the eyes when he talks (and think a sexy thought when you do); this will definitely send him some sexy vibes. When you want to advance the flirtation, touch his arm occasionally, and flirt—in a ladylike way, of course.

Combine Humor with Sensuality

If one did not have a sense of humor, life would be very dreary indeed. Ideally, you want to be entertaining and sensual, though again, in moderation. You want to be a funny, sexy woman; you don't want to be the class clown or someone he doesn't take seriously. Charming is the operative word—be alluring and delightful.

Be a Good Conversationalist

Make intelligent conversation, and accept intelligent conversation in return. Don't be afraid to stimulate the conversation and lead, but make sure you stop short of overpowering him. Men often feel intimidated by overpowering women. (Note: I am saying *overpowering* women, not *powerful* women. Men like women who claim their own power; they do not like women who steamroll over them.)

fabulous quotes

"Give a man a free hand and he will run it all over you."
—Mae West in *Klondike Annie*

Take It Slowly

Walk, don't run into Mr. Right's arms. One-night stands are easy to find everywhere and anywhere—at all hours, with all kinds of men. What you want to do is recognize quality when you see it and then walk into that man's arms. When you know he's the right one for you, just go for it—confidently—but not in a rush.

Don't Be Easy to Get into Bed

Some men can be dogs when it comes to sex; they see no reason to wait until you know each other. And unfortunately, some girls think that because they're big, they should jump on any man that comes around and wants to have some quick sex. Your big size should not be a factor in your quest for a relationship—or for sex. Wait until you know he wants you for you, because he finds *you* attractive and desirable.

let me tell you!

Don't trade sex for affection in a situation where you know that a one-night sex is the target. But if having sex is all you want, then go for it—just remember later that boys will be boys. Don't create a fantasy about him if you knew that all he ever had in mind was hot sex and a goodbye.

Be Sexy, Strut Sexy, Live Sexy

Think of yourself as a voluptuous glamour goddess, as someone who is doubliciously sexy, and walk around letting others know your secret—that you are *all that*, and more. Be a *Size Sexy* goddess and you will attract a man who sees you as a goddess, who really admires you for who you are. He's the man you want to choose for long-term happiness. But remember, he won't know how fabulous you are unless you allow him to see it.

Size Sexy women never have to worry about being attractive. Men love voluptuous and curvaceous women. Just be vivacious, be smart, and be the interesting person that you already are. Bring out your femininity and sensuality. When you walk, when you talk, keep it interesting, keep it sassy, keep it going on. You shouldn't have any kind of a problem.

stella's secrets

I use body language effectively, paired with femininity, to send out sexy and seductive vibes. Know that sexuality and femininity are always expressed through body language and the eyes, but with a delicate touch—be elegant, not vulgar.

Where to Find Men

There are many places where you can meet potential lovers, but make sure you are done up from head to toe, looking and feeling your best, and bringing a sexy, confident, happy vibe along for the ride. Find your man:

- Online
- At a party
- Sitting at an outdoor café
- Browsing in bookstores
- Going out at night on the town with the girls
- In a club, bar or lounge, or restaurant
- While walking in the park on a nice day
- In a supermarket
- While walking your dog
- In a museum or an art gallery
- At the gym

The message: Men are everywhere, ladies, but they're not going to come to you. So, go in search of them. You need to bring your best self forward and let them see who you are and how fabulous you know you are. If you take a little time to look your absolute best and believe in your own attractiveness, they will come like bees to honey! Go out into the world and remember to project a sexy, flirtatious attitude—and to look around for prospects. If you see a man who interests you, don't be afraid to smile and strike up a conversation.

fabulous quotes

"I need sex for a clear complexion, but I'd rather do it for love."
—Joan Crawford

Be Sure to Stay Sexy

One day I went to meet Thierry Mugler for lunch in New York and I did not get all dolled up as usual. I wanted a break from high heels, so I put on sneakers instead. When he first saw me, he looked down at my feet and gave me his Thierry Mugler vicious look (which I happen to love) and then said, " You better put on your high heels girl! They are a part of your personality, sensuality, and character. They keep that voluptuous silhouette in that sexy feminine look." He made it clear that I should stay away from sneakers!

The lesson? Well, as much as I live for getting all dolled up and do believe that *Size Sexy* women—like all women—should look fabulous most of the time, it is also true that you don't ever want to look sloppy. You should always want to look well put together. A few tips for being a daytime diva—in a casual way—follow.

Go Casual with Style

Don't settle for sloppy casual wear. If your sweats are baggy and stained, throw them out and replace them with some stylish casual wear. Keep the bottoms simple, but make sure they flatter your figure. These days many retailers offer fashionable "sweats" in quality fabrics that can even look much better than jeans and a T-shirt. You can also find yoga pants with slightly flared legs that will serve very well for casual wear, as long as you buy them to skim over your curves, not cling. Team them up with zippered jackets, casual sweater sets, or even hoodies, as long as they are tasteful or at least fun. Wear a colorful T-shirt that lights up your face, and add a pair of hoop earrings to help you look more polished.

Pull Your Hair Up

On those days when you don't want to blow out and style your hair, as long as it's clean, you are still good to go. Just pull it up in a sexy ponytail or bun and add a feminine hair accessory. Today you can find many attractive ponytail holders and clips. If your hair is too short to pull up, wear a saucy beret or a cute hat—not a baseball cap!

stella's secrets

On my casual days, I also give my skin a breather. Instead of makeup, I apply nourishing creams that have just a hint of glow for a healthy, pink-in-the-cheeks look.

One Word: Lipstick

Wear lipstick no matter what. You can get away with skipping all the other makeup, but lipstick is a must. It brings color to your face, and it makes you look finished, but not overdone—that's the best trick I have. The choice of lipstick color is up to you—it depends on what is your favorite, what is most flattering on you, what brands you like, and what season it is—that's all up to you. But for me, my color never changes . . . for me, it's always red lipstick.

Wear Sunglasses

The most fabulous accessory is one that will glamorize your casual look, so try putting on a pair of gorgeous sunglasses. Grab a great pair of sunglasses if you're running around in the daytime and, to make sure you look your best, choose a good pair that covers your eyes when you haven't applied makeup or mascara.

Follow the Bare Minimum Rule

Although you can certainly go out in your sunglasses, if you will also be indoors, you might want to practice what I call "bare minimum" glamour. I like to use a little concealer under my eyes, curl my eyelashes, and brush on several coats of mascara. To finish the bare minimum, yet fabulous look, I will also add lipstick (of course, you should always wear lipstick!). You can also use bronzers or skin brighteners to glam up your casual look.

stella's secrets

I know that fashion changes and fades from one style to another, but for me it is always *vive la glamour.* Don't be afraid to be better dressed than anyone else. Be who you want to be. When it comes to glamour, I know one thing for sure: It's me, it's fabulous, and I embrace it!

Evening Casual

You might also find yourself in that situation in the evening where you want to be more casual. Maybe you're going out to meet friends for a relaxing dinner, but you still want to look your best without getting all dolled up. In that case, again, put on a little concealer and a little mascara. Blush and lipstick are also definitely in order. Eye shadow, eyeliner, and foundation are not necessary. Put your hair in a chic chignon. Wear something semi-casual, something that doesn't necessarily show off your curves and something that isn't too baggy, but definitely shows some cleavage. In your wardrobe, always have a couple of tops that you can pair with a simple pair of pants for those kinds of occasions. This is always a nice little evening getaway. Add a nice little bag and you're good to go!

fabulous quotes

"I have always known what I wanted, and that was beauty . . . in every form."
—Joan Crawford

Nighttime Diva: The Queen of the Night

Nighttime is the most fun time to dress up, because you know you're going to have fun, party, meet new people, fall in love, and enhance the romance that's already in your life. It's about fabulous dinners with friends or glamorous cocktail parties. The hair and makeup is done to the nines, the clothing is sexy, revealing, and sensual, and high heels are a must.

Nighttime is also the time when you pull out all of your jewels, your accessories, your wonderful bags, and your sexiest lingerie. And it's when people are usually in their most relaxed environment; they're looser and more ready for fun. Even if you're going out with business acquaintances or with your husband to a work event, people are more relaxed and ready to have a good time. It's a great way to get to know people from your nightlife that could become involved in your day life.

Nighttime is absolutely the best time of the day for me—it is when I glow—and you can too. It's a time when your sassy, fun, and funky personality can come out without any boundaries. Your self-confidence has a 100 percent chance for exposure. But these can also be the self-acceptance moments that challenge you. When you go out at night, you don't want to be covering up or wearing loose clothing; this is the time when you let it all out. This is the time when you get the most opportunities to make the grand entrance. Next, we'll discuss a few tips for being the queen of the night.

*fabulous*quotes

"Even when we wear nothing, our clothes are talking noisily to everyone who sees us . . . unless we are naked and bald, it is impossible to be silent."
—Alison Lurie, Author of *The Language of Clothes*

Dress Appropriately

Make sure that you know the dress code, so to speak, for the occasion, the kind of event and venue you're going to. Whether you will be hopping from one club to another, going out with girlfriends for a few drinks, or heading out with a few friends to a fabulous, trendy restaurant, just take care with how you dress; a lot of women have the tendency—because it's nighttime and things are a little looser—to get lost and forget that there's a thin line between sexy and slutty, and overexpose themselves. You always want to hold yourself in a proper, but still sexy and sensual, manner.

On the other hand, you also want to make sure that you are dressed up enough. If you are going to a dressy event, don't be afraid to wear your best attire—this is the time to put on that eye-popping dress so that all eyes are on you. For these occasions, go the extra mile to be a glamorous nighttime diva.

Make an Entrance

Making an entrance, especially at night, is a great moment of positive acknowledgment. To make an entrance, you must be done up to the nines with a look and an attitude that no one can ignore. Let your beauty and femininity shine! Walk tall and proud. And go for it! When you pull it off, the feedback you will get from other people will leave you feeling amazing. You will wonder why you waited so long to make your grand entrance!

Be Charming

One should always be charming, of course. When you know that you will be attending an event with a lot of politicians, for example, study up on politics so you can dazzle them with your intelligence. When you are attending a party to celebrate, be fun and bubbly and hold up your end of the conversation with people. Everyone is attracted to an interesting woman, so let them know that you are someone whose company they would enjoy. And don't be afraid to shake that booty on the dance floor!

stella's secrets

Nighttime is one of my favorite dressing times of the day because there are many more categories in which you can be creative: special occasion, casual evening, glamorous evening, sexy evening, evening formal, evening chic. Nighttime is the perfect time to shine.

Underwear? Under There!

A lot of women focus on outerwear and ignore undergarments. That's a shame, not only because they can be among the prettiest, most luxurious items in your wardrobe, but also because how well your undergarments fit you affects how well your outfits fit you—and how confident you'll be when impressing your man.

Take, for instance, the bra and other support garments, which are the cornerstones of any fabulous look you're trying to create. Do yours fit properly?

Are they supportive and comfortable? Do they enhance your best features? Do you know the different kinds of support garments?

When it comes to undergarments, there are a number of "must-haves" for *Size Sexy* women and we'll talk about them here. Keep in mind that, when choosing any undergarment, you not only want to support and flatter your body, but you also want to create a feeling of being sexy for you and for your paramour.

Underwire Bras

Underwire bras are the best bras for good, solid support. The trick is that they must be well constructed and cut in the heart shape. They should go low, with a narrow connection in the front. That is very important for a low décolletage. Look for bras with extra padding over the underwires to ensure your comfort no matter where the night—or day—takes you.

Push-up Bras

Push-up bras are great for making those babies rise up! The trick is to buy them one size smaller in the cup. This will really give you the ultimate drop-dead cleavage and will make clothes look better, particularly fitted tops or wrap dresses.

The Padded Bra

For those of you who are not blessed enough on top, the padded bra is here to help. The trick is that the padded bra will make you look a little fuller, a little bigger, without having breast implant surgery. They will also help you balance your bosom with your hips and make clothing look better on your frame. Some now come with padding on the sides so it pushes your breasts up and together, helping a small-busted woman look well endowed.

Cinchers or Nippers

I'm talking about old-fashioned corset-like cinchers that don't connect to your bra. There are two sizes of them: one that sits below the bra and goes to the waist; and one that sits just on the waist. The trick for the first one is to push the boobs up while narrowing the waist. The trick for the second one is to cinch your waist. There are also more modern versions of these garments, some which are connected to high panties, so it comes all in one piece, and they are fantastic. They can be found in lingerie and specialty stores, and they really are a blessing for both *Size Sexy* girls and skinny women who need help enhancing their curves.

fabulous quotes

"I didn't discover curves, I only uncovered them."
—Mae West

High-Waist Tummy Control

High-waist tummy control is one of the most important shapers that a *Size Sexy* woman should have in her arsenal. This shaper is for the days when your hormones and your monthly cycles are controlling your body or even when your stomach is just a little bloated. It is the perfect shaper to help you to keep or create a smooth silhouette.

Spandex Undergarments

When you are wearing clothes that fit close to your body, such as wrap dresses or blouses, sweaters, knits, or jersey pants, dresses, or skirts, it is always wise to wear a body sleeker—one of the many spandex shapers that will minimize cellulite and help your clothes glide over your curves. Once you find a brand that works for your body and that you can wear for long periods of time, buy them in beige and black, with sexy lace trimming, or whatever you prefer—whatever helps you feel sexier. Beige and black will work for almost everything you wear, but it's fun to add other colors when you can afford to spice up your undergarment wardrobe. If you have a slender torso, you may even be able to get away with just wearing pantyhose.

stella's secrets

The ultimate body shapers are corsets under your clothing, but who can support *them* for more than one hour? One trick to use is to wear support pantyhose, as long as they hold the whole leg and thighs in a solid, smooth look and give good support.

Lingerie

One of the many ways to show off your sensuality, femininity, and sexuality in private is by wearing feminine, sexy lingerie. So, something the new *Size Sexy* you might want to do is go out and buy yourself a new, hot, seductive set of lingerie, because feeling feminine and sexy is where it all begins! The Internet is a good source for lingerie and undergarments for the full-figured goddess, while Fredericks of Hollywood is always a reliable source for lacy, racy, sexy wear.

And don't wait until you have a man in your life—wear them now, wear them for you, wear them to pamper your inner *Size Sexy* woman. If you need more reasons to embrace sexy feminine lingerie, know that there are many ways it can factor into your wardrobe. Wear lingerie:

- As your sleepwear, lingerie gives you a great, comforting feeling of softness.
- To make you even more desirable, sexy, and seductive to your partner, making it more fun and kinky in the bedroom.

- For your own pleasure under your outfits, just to have that feeling of smooth silkiness against your skin and to enhance your feelings of femininity. Don't deprive yourself of that pleasure just because there isn't a man in the picture.

The options are endless. You have styles of lingerie that range from sweet and feminine to a sexy doll to fantasy and fetish designs. Whatever turns you on, just be a lingerie goddess.

It Bears Repeating: You Are Sexy and Fabulous

Basically, every day when you get dressed and look at yourself in your mirror, being a *Size Sexy* woman should be something you not only accept, but something you embrace and love about yourself. When you go to the grocery store, out to dinner with your friends, to the salon for a manicure, or to a grand cocktail party, you should always project yourself as a confident, self-accepting, sexy, and fabulous woman.

In fact, repeat that to yourself: You are a confident, self-accepting, sexy, and fabulous woman. There is always room for improvement—nobody's perfect—but no one else should dictate to you what or who or how you will be, or what or how you will look or behave.

One more time: You are a confident, self-accepting, sexy, and fabulous woman—a *Size Sexy* woman—and you needn't look any further than your own mirror to find the most important person in the world who should tell you that!

Fine-Tuning

As we approach the end of this journey together, we're really delving into the fun parts—and pampering yourself is discussed in the next chapter. But have you learned the important lessons found in this chapter?

Hopefully, you have taken the following lessons to heart and realize that:

- It is okay to initiate a flirt as long as it is done gracefully.
- Body language is universal, so speak with confidence!
- Don't waste your time with men who do not appreciate you!
- Be casual but with style!
- Find yourself a pair of fashionable sunglasses!
- Nighttime is fun time for dressing up.
- Making an entrance creates a first impression—make it a positive one.
- Wearing lingerie is sensual and feminine.
- Body shapers are a *must*!
- Remember: You are sexy and fabulous!

chapter **nine**

pamper your *self*

One of the best ways that a *Size Sexy* woman can show respect and love for herself is to pamper herself by grooming her hair, her skin, her hands, her feet, and her body. Hair is a woman's crowning glory and is one of the best assets you have to flaunt. Your skin must last a lifetime, and the better it looks, the happier you will be. Your hands and feet are two places where you really show how much you value your attractiveness. And your body is your temple! All of these are not only crucial to your happiness, but grooming them can make you feel and look fabulous—and isn't that what being *Size Sexy* is all about? Of course it is!

Grooming Your Hair

It is very important that you choose a hairstyle that flatters your face shape, your neck, and your body. My first and utmost recommendation for finding your perfect hairstyle is to schedule a consultation with a professional. They will help match you with the best cut, style, and color for your hair type, hair condition, face, body, and lifestyle.

The shape and style of your hair are the next important things. How do I know this? Well, my husband Dov is an amazing hairstylist, which is so fortunate for me. I am a lucky woman indeed to have my own personal stylist!

stella's secrets

Make sure you tell your stylist about who you are, your lifestyle, what activities you're involved with, and so on. All this information will help the stylist determine what cut, style, and color will work best for you.

A word of caution about hairstyling that goes along with what I've said about blindly following fashion trends. Trends in hairstyles, as with fashion, are great, but one trend does not necessarily fit all sizes and shapes. Instead, work toward finding the style that is right for you and that looks good on your face shape. Also, make sure that the style you choose is right for you and will fit in with your lifestyle, your job, and the clothes you like to wear. A good stylist who's taken the time to get to know a bit about you and what you want will be able to help you find the right style. Remember, every *Size Sexy* woman owes it to herself to look stylish and up to date.

A good stylist can also give you valuable tips about your hair color. He or she will let you know what color matches your skin tone, what color you can maintain easily, and which color will relate to your personality.

Hairstyle Tips

There are certain basics that women should take into account when making hairstyle choices and taking care of their hair. Keep the following in mind:

- Not a lot of women can get away with really short hair, because the style and cut should be proportionate to your body. That's especially true for *Size Sexy* women.

- Treat your hair with the same care you treat your face—give yourself moisturizing masques and don't over-treat your locks with chemicals. In fact, it's best not to experiment at home with hair chemicals if you don't know what you're doing. Chemicals can damage your hair's health and an amateur hair treatment will almost always *look* like an amateur hair treatment.
- Sometimes the color we're born with isn't the one that looks best on us, so feel free to change it up. Try not to do the coloring and highlight treatments at home. Again, it's best to leave chemical changes to professionals.
- High ponytails are always good for women with larger shapes. I love to have my hair up and high when I go out at night, and a high ponytail will always be in proportion with the rest of my body. And nothing makes you feel better about yourself than knowing that you are glamorous and sexy!
- A chignon, or a bun, is a good look for almost any *Size Sexy* woman.
- Good hair volume on top is always good for the *Size Sexy* girl, because it helps you create an elongated look. It's also very important to have hair in proportion to the rest of your body
- Keep your hair off your face. This helps keep your face open. You want your hair to frame your face, but not close it off.
- If you have a square, big face, bangs tend to square it off even more; be sure you have the right facial shape to carry them.
- Deep treatment conditioner is essential for keeping hair healthy. Whether you choose a hot or cold treatment, you can do it at home or pamper yourself and have one done at a salon.

The most important thing, of course, is that you should feel feminine and sexy with your hairstyle. And the best way to go about getting that beautiful, flattering style is to put your hair in the hands of professionals, who match your look with your personality, your lifestyle, and the rest of your body.

let me tell you!

I am a BBBB and I want you to be a happy BBBB too—a Big, Beautiful, Bodacious Babe.

Choose Someone You Trust—and Like

Always either go to a stylist who comes highly recommended, or to someone who can show you examples of his or her work on other peoples' hair, but whichever you choose, make sure the person you see is someone you feel comfortable interacting with. Again, your stylist should understand what you want. A good stylist may also have a better idea about what would be the best look for you, or they can help you find a totally new style that will bring more sparkle to your look and help you showcase your fun and positive attitude.

However, choosing a stylist can be intimidating because this is what they do all day and, when they are good, they tend to develop a good eye—and strong opinions about what would look best on their clients. If you don't feel comfortable with a stylist, chances are that you are not going to walk out of that salon feeling happy with your hair. This is very important when you have a consultation. And don't be shy or embarrassed to just let the stylist know if you don't think you are on the same page and you won't be using his or her services; just politely tell him it's not a good match and look for someone who feels right for you. Just make sure you are comfortable talking to the stylist that you choose and that you trust him to carry out your wishes.

*fabulous*quotes

"Luxury is the necessity that begins where necessity ends."
—Coco Chanel

Be Creative with Your Hair

Don't just stick to one look and wear it all the time. Have fun! Try on different looks occasionally. When you change outfits, try to match your hair with that new you. It's fun!

I myself wear a lot of hairpieces, although I have very healthy and long hair. Again, I'm lucky enough to have a talented husband who creates these gorgeous pieces for me. With these hairpieces, it takes no time to get ready because good hairpieces will blend right in with your own hair. They allow me to go from drab to fab in seconds. If I have to enhance my hairdo to make it look a little bigger or fuller, or to create different looks and styles, all those hairpieces are perfect. It makes life so much easier when getting ready for occasions that require me to be done up—and they can do the same for you, too.

stella's secrets

I highly recommend those amazing hairpieces that will allow you to be ready to go in a snap, whether you're having a good hair day or bad hair day. For more information, visit Dov's Salon in New York City, or the salon website at *www.dovhair.com.*

Grooming Your Hands and Feet

As I have already mentioned several times, grooming is a very important part of any woman's beauty routine. Big or small, women should spend time pampering their hands and feet, keeping them immaculately groomed and not only presentable, but very attractive.

Pamper Your Hands!

Hands are always visible so it is crucial that you spend time making sure yours are manicured and pretty. Your hands are the first part of the body that people notice, and they are in motion all the time, so groom and lotion them religiously. Here are some golden rules about grooming hands:

- Make sure your hands are well manicured and well moisturized.
- If you have problems with nail growth, use treatments, or use fake nails.
- Wraps and acrylics are the best, and a little length looks good on every woman.

- Having clean, nicely shaped and polished nails with a little length is an essential part of having your whole look together, and I don't know why some women underestimate that. It's a very feminine thing.

stella's secrets

It's important to indulge and pamper yourself; it's a key part of creating a new, confident you. Taking care of yourself by doing things like getting a good hair and makeup consultation is a good investment in the most important thing in your life—*you!*—and is a major part of creating your personal style.

Pamper Your Feet!

Pedicures are also a must. You can pay your feet less attention during the winter because you will be wearing shoes most of the time, but that still doesn't mean your feet should be neglected. Here are my favorite tips when it comes to pampering feet:

- I believe in giving the toenails a break from polish, because when you do paint them all the time they tend to get discolored. Winter is the perfect time to treat your feet for the indoors—moisturize them to the max with socks and lotions.
- Lotions are the best way to get nice soft heels. The heels can become so dry and cracked that your feet look like the Sahara desert. And that is not only unattractive, but it's also painful.
- Another luxurious treat for your feet is a paraffin wax treatment, which are available at a lot of manicure places. You can also buy the machine for home use. I have one and I love it. It feels wonderful and, by the time summer comes around, your feet will look pretty and be all ready for lovely heels and sandals and wearing colors on your toes.
- Remember, don't neglect your feet; they're what carry you to greatness!

Pamper Your Skin!

Ladies, remember that your facial skin is very important. So clean it, care for it, and nourish it. A lot of women tend to think it's not an important issue, but trust me—it's actually *very* important. You want to have shiny, flawless, radiant skin that shows you pamper and take good care of it. The only way you can achieve that is by taking care of your face. Clean your skin and keep it nourished.

To do that, you have to pick the lotions, creams, and makeup that is best for you. That's easy enough to do: Go to those wonderful cosmetic counters in department stores and take recommendations from them. Shop around; don't feel pressured to buy at the first counter you go to. Ask for samples and take them home and try them out.

It is very important to have a morning cleansing routine for your face—feel free to use some kind of soap, but again, make sure it's appropriate for you and your skin type. Younger skin may need soaps that soak up any excess oil; more mature skin may want soap with emollients and special ingredients to add moisture. Some skins cannot tolerate soap and will find even the most gentle brand irritating.

The best bet is to get recommendations from a cosmetic specialist, but don't let her oversell you things you don't need or convince you to buy the most expensive products. Very often you can find the same ingredients or properties in less-expensive products. But wherever, or whatever you buy, make sure you include these essentials in your skin-care routine:

- A morning cleanser
- Eye cream
- Neck cream
- A daytime moisturizer
- Serum
- Eye makeup remover
- Makeup remover
- Cleansing lotion
- Lip moisturizer
- Nighttime moisturizer

- Toner
- A good hydration mask

Again, all of these products should be specific for your skin type. You can use the same eye cream for daytime and nighttime, but you may need a special moisturizer for night. Nighttime moisturizers are a lot thicker and are more moisturizing for the skin.

These are the steps that are important to any woman, of any size or age, for keeping your skin in good health. I also recommend using creams that include at least an SPF 15 or 20, because then you know that your skin has some basic protection from the sun when you're walking around during the day.

let me tell you!

Each and every woman, no matter what age and size, should have a personal esthetician and get facials as often as needed.

How else can you pamper your skin? Here are a few skin do's and don'ts:

- Do remove makeup, cleanse, and moisturize your face before bed. It is important to clean your face after being out, whether you were wearing makeup or not.
- Don't go to bed with your makeup on. Going to sleep with makeup on is a big no-no! You'll feel terrible when you wake up in the morning, with makeup smudged all over your skin and all over your pillow. Your skin will also be dry and irritable, and you will not feel good. And it's just terribly unhealthy for your skin—even a little bit of mascara is not good to leave on.

*fabulous*quotes

"Like anyone else, there are days I feel beautiful, and there are days I don't. And when I don't, I do something about it."
—Cheryl Tiegs

Embrace Makeup

Every woman can improve her look with makeup. Some have flawless skin and are able to wear minimal makeup and look fabulous; others require the assistance of makeup to highlight their best features. Everyone can benefit from a little eye shadow, blush, mascara, and lipstick.

To apply makeup, make sure you have makeup that protects your skin and matches your coloring, basic sets of makeup tools, and a nice, relaxing place to apply your makeup. I have a beautiful vanity table, which is truly my self-pampering spot. It's my beauty shrine, and I love it. I have pictures around it to inspire me. I like to keep my makeup area nice and clean, spacious with a good-sized mirror, lights around the mirror—because that's my special place. Every woman should create that for herself, a private area where it's just you, yourself, and your tools. Speaking of tools, the art of applying makeup requires its own set of special tools, so let's discuss what you need to create a beautiful face.

The Essentials of a Good Set of Makeup Tools

The following is a list of the tools that are necessary to apply makeup effectively and evenly:

- *Eyelash comb:* This is good for making sure you have no clumps in your eyelashes when you apply mascara.
- *Powder brush:* A huge powder brush is good to use after you've done your makeup and after you've powdered; it will help you remove all the excess powder.
- *Blush brush:* Another large brush that helps you apply your blush. One tip: Be conservative when using the brush, because it can pick up too much blush. Give it a good shake when you take the blush from the compact. To use, start at the center of your cheekbone and go up toward the lower part of your temple to accentuate your cheekbones.

- *Lip brush:* Usually very smooth and flat. You can apply your lipstick with it if you don't want to apply it directly from the tube.
- *Two kinds of sponges:* The round ones and the wedge sponges. Use whichever you prefer for applying foundation and for blending and powdering your face.
- *An eyelash curler:* It's a must! It opens the lashes and makes your eyes look more open.
- *Eyebrow brush:* It smoothes down the hairs and helps shape your brows, and also smoothes out and blends eyebrow pencil marks.
- *Contour brush:* Basically a very good tool in making changes once you've applied makeup. It accentuates and minimizes various parts of the face.
- *Tweezers:* For plucking your eyebrows. If you can do a good job yourself, do it. If not, it is easy to find a good eyebrow artist or a great eyebrow kit to help you find the perfect shape for your brows. Don't just go to anyone, however—go to someone reputable.
- *A pair of small scissors:* Good for when you are shaping your brows. Sometimes you don't want to pluck, but you may need to do a little trimming on some wayward brow hairs.

stella's secrets

It is very important to have good-quality brushes—natural fiber, mink, or sable are best—and to keep the brushes clean, because they collect bacteria very quickly. Clean them at least once a week, using a light shampoo or some rubbing alcohol.

Consult an Expert

My best recommendation to each and every one of you *Size Sexy* ladies is to give yourself the gift of a consultation with a professional makeup artist. There are a lot of very talented makeup artists out there—a lot of the department stores have top-notch professionals at their cosmetics counters.

My basic makeup collection is a mixture of several different brands, but your collection should be made up of your favorites. Shop around—and remember, the department store makeup counters will be happy to help you find which products are best for you. Most of them will even do free makeovers and may offer you samples you can try at home. This is a valuable and fun service, and it is really a great way to pamper yourself.

stella's secrets

When it comes to makeup, I say less is more, depending on the occasion. I don't like to see women wearing too much makeup in the middle of the day or young, beautiful faces that have been covered up by all the color that has been applied.

Select the Right Colors

One of the best tips when it comes to makeup is to take the time to select colors that are right for your skin, coloring, and eyes. A makeup expert can be invaluable in helping you determine the ideal colors for you; but don't be afraid to experiment. With foundation, you should match it as closely as possible to your skin so you can blend it in and make it invisible to the naked eye. When it comes to lipstick and eye shadow, you have more leeway to play with color. Younger women are free to play with color; more mature women may want to steer clear of bright colors—go for more subtle matte finish shades. This also applies to eyeliner, which looks fabulous on eyes; it can help make your eyes look bigger and more catlike. If applied correctly, eyeliner can lift mature and droopy eyes.

A few words on makeup colors:

- Try to stick to the colors of the season. They do change from winter to spring to summer to fall, but only follow those suggestions if the current colors match your face and style.

- There are also color trends. Check them out, but as with all other trends related to fashion, follow them only if they look good on *you*!
- You can also mix a couple of colors of makeup to create a custom blend for yourself.
- Heavy eye makeup and glittery eye shadow are good for nighttime and party time.

stella's secrets

Going out at night offers the perfect opportunity to play a little with makeup. You can experiment with colors and style and have fun with it, because that's the time to wear a little more. Whatever suits your face, the occasion, and your personality is best!

The Essentials of a Good Makeup Bag

These will be the items that you always carry in your handbag. Buy yourself a pretty makeup bag and place the following items in it:

- Mascara: There are good products at the drug store and at the cosmetic counters, so you don't necessarily need to spend a lot of money on mascara. Try a couple before deciding on your brand.
- Foundation: Find the right shade for your skin tone and choose the one that feels best on your skin.
- Concealer: Eye concealer is very important. In fact, it's a must.
- Blush
- Eyebrow pencil or powder pencil
- A couple of shades of eye shadow
- Lip pencil
- Lip gloss: It's a quicker picker upper—it can really make a look!
- Translucent powder

- A variety of colors of lipsticks: You should have a day look and a nighttime look, just as you do with your clothes.

stella's secrets

I believe in having a wardrobe of perfumes. I have daytime perfume for summer and winter, and I have nighttime for summer and winter. I find the perfumes and the oils of the body mix differently during the different seasons. For instance, in the summer, heavy and sweet perfumes can be a little too much, while in the winter, that same scent can be perfect for a night on the town. I like to keep it light and flowery during the day.

Take Your *Size Sexy* Self to a Spa

Becoming a *Size Sexy* woman means you have to stop giving yourself reasons to *not* do the things you want to do in your life—like, for instance, indulging yourself with a fabulous day at the spa!

Going to a spa can be something that is very hard for a lot of women, of all sizes. Some women worry about having to get disrobed, about not being comfortable getting a massage, even about details like whether or not there will be robes to fit them. But trust me, a day of pampering yourself and treating your body, mind, and spirit to the kind of luxurious treatments you'll get during a day at the spa more than make up for any fears you may have.

let me tell you!

You are not alone. Do you know how many times I have been on and off the wagon of weight loss? I can't even count anymore. Even though I was never skinny, I have always looked good and felt good, no matter what size I was. And that is okay by me.

A few tips to help you make the most of your spa day include:

- Plan a great day of treatments with a friend who will not only share the experience, but will also help you feel more comfortable and relaxed.
- Arrive for your appointment fifteen to twenty minutes early to give yourself a chance to become acquainted with the spa layout, the changing area, and, of course, the menu of fabulous treatments.
- Most spas do offer larger-sized robes. But if you want to make sure you have everything you need to make the most of your day, call ahead to check, or simply take your own clean, white, and luxurious robe.
- In addition to the menu of services, make sure you ask about all the other amenities at the spa. Many offer Jacuzzis, saunas, steam rooms, massages, reading materials, personal music players, and other small touches that will make your day extra special.
- Book a couple of different treatments. A new you means trying new things, and the spa is the perfect place to do that. Try a body wrap and scrub, a facial, a manicure and pedicure, a wax treatment . . . anything that you think will have you leaving the spa feeling even more *Size Sexy* fabulous!

Enjoy a Massage

One treatment that you simply must try during a spa day is a massage. I know this can be incredibly intimidating if you are shy about your body, but the payoff is worth it.

A lot of women, of all shapes and sizes, are especially uncomfortable with having a man massage their body, but from my personal experience, I can tell you that it is the way to go. I really love deep-tissue massages and, because men are stronger, they can really get their hands on your skin and help you release all the tension. This is an experience that is a tremendous release from being uptight and uncomfortable and I really think every woman should try it.

The first few minutes of your massage may be uncomfortable, but then you should just dive in and let yourself go. Trust me, you will forget about any discomfort once you make up your mind to relax. Break all the barriers you've set for yourself and try it! This is the time to test yourself and try new things. Forget about covering up and being shy.

If you simply can't get relaxed with the thought of a massage from a male masseuse, no worries, just ask for a female masseuse. And if the idea of a full-body massage is just too much for your visit, you can always start with a neck and shoulder massage or a reflexology treatment.

The point is simply to treat yourself to a day of beauty and feeling fabulous. The way you choose to go about that will depend on your comfort level. Also remember:

- If you don't want to go to a spa, many gyms offer massage services and even treatments like reflexology sessions.
- A lot of masseuses will make house calls, which might also be a way to try a massage in a setting and circumstance that will allow you to be more relaxed.
- The fun of spa day shouldn't end when you leave the spa. After your massage, you're going to be so relaxed, so radiant, that I suggest you relax with a wonderful dinner in a restaurant that you never dared going into for one reason or another. Maybe choose a place with gourmet cuisine! But wherever you choose to go, make sure you take the time to indulge, have fun, and get a great bottle of wine.

I hope you are starting to feel the change and are running toward the new *Size Sexy* woman you are becoming. Your new look, your new self confidence, the new you who is breaking through all of your old barriers is a *Size Sexy* woman who's going to begin enjoying her life!

chapter **ten**

expand your *self*

You're almost there—we've reached the final chapter on your road to becoming a *Size Sexy* woman. It is time to take your image of what it means to be a full-figured woman to another level, to take responsibility for accepting yourself and approaching your life with a positive attitude. Imagine how great it will be to feel relief from the bondage of low self-esteem and how you'll feel when you are finally able to stop being a prisoner of society and the media's images of how women are supposed to look, feel, and think. I'm not suggesting that this book has magically fixed all that troubles you. But I do hope it has helped you muster up enough courage to become a happy, fabulous, self-accepting *Size Sexy* woman. A healthy way to live in life, regardless of your size and your shape, is to be connected to yourself and to your being—your physical, mental, and spiritual being—and that takes work. Life is not just about size and beauty; there are things that are more important, deeper than those things.

let me tell you

Jean Paul Gaultier said to me, "You don't belong backstage, you belong on stage." The same applies to you so step out and stop hiding!

Expand Your Vision of Your *Self*

Your size is not all that you are. I didn't become a high-fashion personality and model based solely on my looks. Gaultier and Mugler chose me based on how I looked and how I felt about myself. My looks, my personality, my confidence, and my *Size Sexy* attitude created the attraction. If I had just been a big girl or someone with a pretty face, I could have walked down the street and no one would have noticed me. I could have continued working as a makeup artist, and I would have been someone who happened to work in the fashion industry.

Be Your Sassy Self

Because I felt such love for myself, exuded such confidence, and projected that confidence outward, people—fashion people—noticed. It was about the way I looked, the way I walked, the way I represented myself. My magnetic, sassy personality made the biggest names in the fashion industry take notice and want to put everything that was Stella on display in a larger arena. That totality of Stella is what they were really embracing, and it felt so good.

stella's secrets

Attractiveness is all about how you represent yourself, how you look, how you dress, how you carry yourself, how fabulous you are in your own world, in your own ways—that is what really matters, what makes other people respect and admire you.

Size ceased to be an issue. I was simply there, part of the scene, and all the fashion insiders considered me to be this fabulous, beautiful woman, just as I was, no questions asked. And that's where all full-figured women should strive to find ourselves: at a place where you can confidently, boldly say to the world, "This is it, this *is* me!" The size you wear should not be an issue.

Let the Old Obsessions Go

When it comes to focusing on your dress size, just break free of that limited thinking; let the old obsessions go. Start concentrating on developing and showcasing other aspects of who you are that will fully express what is special about you. That's what I did, and if it worked for me, it will work for you. I didn't focus on my size, and that led me to becoming part of a world that included Linda Evangelista, Naomi Campbell, Kate Moss, Christy Turlington, Tyra Banks, Stephanie Seymour, Cindy Crawford, and a lot of other fabulous models. I was no more, or no less, a part of that scene than any of those famous supermodels. Well, except for maybe the difference of a few pounds—and a few magazine covers!

let me tell you!

Every woman, regardless of size, shape, or age, has body issues—even those gorgeous models who you think should have nothing to complain about often feel as if they have problem areas.

Liberate Your *Self*: Your Weight Is Not All That You Are

Not everyone is meant to be the same size, even from a health perspective. We all have different body types and shapes. This should be an important factor in helping you become comfortable with your body and obtaining what I conceptualize as "freedom of size." When you have, or adopt, a freedom of size attitude, it means you feel comfortable in your skin, with your body, and that you will not allow what other people—be they people you know, strangers, the media, or societal attitudes—affect how you think or feel about your own body. Cast all those negative thoughts aside and focus only on what *you* think of yourself.

Build up a healthy dose of self-esteem, engage in an active social life, and go out and enjoy yourself. It is for you to enjoy, not for anyone else to knock down. And when people see you living your life to the fullest, they may change their limited attitudes about *Size Sexy* women.

fabulous quotes

"How dare anybody try to tell me what I should look like or what I should be when there is so much more to me than just my weight?"
—America Ferrera in *Real Women Have Curves*

Change Your Thinking Now!

Imagine all the great things this change in attitude will make, how quickly it will lead to a happier you. Like many full-figured women, you may have spent your whole life trying to be thin and putting everything else on hold. If this is the case, it's time to surrender that mindset and focus your self-improvement effort elsewhere. But not on the weight issues, especially if your body has the tendency to gain quickly: You know only too well that you will lose a few pounds and you will gain a few pounds. Try not to gain too much—keep your body at a comfortable size, *Size Sexy*—but go out and find yourself a fabulous lifestyle now—not later, now!

As soon as you begin your quest for a more exciting life and focus on what will help you expand your whole being, you can begin to release yourself from both the pressure that you put on yourself and the pressure others put on you to have a skinny body. Don't ever let anyone tell you that you cannot be beautiful otherwise. By now, hopefully, you know in your heart and mind that this is totally false.

Eliminate all obstacles that prevent you from accepting the positive you, the feminine you, the sexy you, and the self-accepting you, and—last but not least—the new beautiful you with a new attitude on living life as a full-figured, positive, sexy, vibrant, and powerful babe.

stella's secrets

Like a lot of full-figured women, I bet that you spend too much time fretting about your weight and tend to make it the central focus of your life—perhaps so much so that you simply forget to *enjoy* your life. One of the best, most important pieces of advice I can give you: Don't make that mistake for one more day! Enjoy your life, starting now, starting wherever you are.

Act Now!

I'd like you to know that you—and only you—can make a difference for yourself. To make the difference is to take all the elements we've talked about in the book and start making the change. Start doing things you have never dared to do before, maybe things that you were depriving yourself of because you thought you were too full-figured to pursue them.

I hope you take all those fears and hesitations that kept you from living the life you want to live and throw them away. Become a strong woman, a woman of style, because life is short—and this life is yours and nobody else's. You're supposed to dictate for yourself how you're going to live it, how you're going to look, and what you're going to do with your life. Starting to create that new woman that you will become, the self-accepting woman that you are going to become, isn't going to happen overnight, but it will be worth the time and effort you put into it. Here are a few encouraging reminders to help you:

- Find your *Size Sexy* comfort zone. Being comfortable is essential for feeling confident.
- Remember, happiness does not come in a dress size. Create your own happiness—no matter how full-figured you are!

- Work on your attitude. Attitude affects how you approach your life and how you treat yourself and others. Remember, a positive attitude looks good on everyone!
- Take action! You can be and you should be that talented, vibrant, intelligent, sassy, and fabulous *Size Sexy* woman that you truly are. Make up your mind and become her!

stella's secrets

Accept your *Size Sexy*, full-figured, beautiful self, and be happy. If you're not happy, make the change now. Lose weight, change your appearance, change the things about yourself, inside and out, that you are not happy with, and become the fabulous woman you know you truly are.

Become Your *Size Sexy* Self More Fully: Seek Inner Beauty

It's also important to focus on your inner beauty. You'll feel better about your whole package if you're not focusing solely on your looks. Read books about different things to enhance your interests, to become an intelligent, sophisticated woman, and to learn more about the world. Books about art, photography, literature, fashion, history, or anything else that will enrich your personal knowledge will make you more interested in the world around you—and more interesting to the people you meet! Here are a few ideas:

- Visit art galleries and study art history.
- Take a history class and visit historical sites.
- Travel to a foreign country and study the language and culture beforehand.
- Read political magazines or websites to be up-to-date on what's happening in the world.

- Take a class to learn a new skill—cooking, painting, photography, fashion design, calligraphy, sculpting, glass-blowing, interior design, architecture, investing, and so on.
- Volunteer to work for a cause that excites you.
- Join social clubs.
- Sign up for a wine appreciation class.
- Enhance your current professional skills.
- Start your own book club, fashion society, poetry reading, or historical society.

Your goal should be to get to a place where you know you are a beautiful woman, inside and out.

fabulous quotes

"It is confidence in our bodies, minds and spirits that allows us to keep looking for new adventures, new directions to grow in, and new lessons to learn—which is what life is all about."
—Oprah Winfrey

Be Good to Your Self

I'm sure there will be days when you feel a little down, uncomfortable, or even unhappy with your shape. That's okay. We all have those days, no matter what size or shape we are. Things will not change in one day, and you do not need to be a superwoman. Every woman regardless of size, shape, or weight has body issues and days when she feels down, uncomfortable, unhappy with her shape. We all experience them. We all have those days when nothing we wear looks good and we feel stuck in a totally negative body image. So let's bring in a little reality check to make you realize that your negative body image is in your head and you are allowing it to erode your entire positive attitude and your high self-esteem. Try to break out of those days whenever possible. Here are some tips and inspiration to help you out.

Be Realistic

Only compare yourself against yourself. Don't allow yourself to become obsessed with the images of models or actresses that you see in those glamorous magazines, women that look microscopically small compared to you. Sometimes if you see some of those models and actresses in real life, even they don't look like themselves. When those photographs are taken—by accomplished photographers who know how to make everyone look fantastic by the way—those models are surrounded by hair and makeup people who have a talent for making anyone look beautiful, and they have the benefit of fabulous clothes, great lighting, and computer retouching, in which a skilled artisan sculpts their image. I'm not saying that those women are not beautiful; I'm just saying that they get a lot of help that makes them look so perfect. And remember, we're all built differently, and I say *vive la difference.*

let me tell you

I'm not saying that those bodylicious Victoria's Secret hot-and-steamy-looking girls are not sexy. I'm just saying that we are bodylicious, hot and steamy *Size Sexy*, Stella's Secret girls.

Surely by now you realize that these women are either born with a narrow frame and a superhuman metabolism or they starve themselves. Save yourself a lot of unnecessary and unproductive grief and don't compare yourself to women who have completely different body types and shapes. Don't pick an unrealistic standard that you cannot measure up to. Try to limit any comparisons to your own true, realistic, comfortable size.

let me tell you!

Focus on what makes you feel good and create your own reality.

Be Positive

If you are feeling down, it's time to rediscover positive and beautiful things about your body and your face—and I'm sure there are a lot of them. Make a list of your assets and post it on your mirror so you can see them every day. Focus on the aspects of your beauty and your personality that are fabulous and allow those thoughts to overpower any negative feelings. Repeat after me: "I am fabulous—just the way I am. My face reflects my inner beauty, and my body is voluptuous and alluring. I am fabulously feminine and attractive." You get the point—make your own list and believe it!

*fabulous*quotes

"I really don't know how to be anyone else, and whenever I try to be anyone else, I fail miserably. Or I disappoint myself. It doesn't build my self-esteem, and it doesn't help me grow me at all."
—Queen Latifah

Be Inquisitive

If you are really having a hard time seeing the beautiful side of yourself, and you have friends, family, or lovers around, ask them to point out the qualities and attributes of your body that they see, love, and admire. Sometimes what you don't like about your shape may be precisely what they love the most! When they begin sharing how much they love and admire your appearance, listen to them—they are not lying to you. It's you who has been lying to yourself by thinking so many negative thoughts. Sometimes every woman needs her closest friends and family to remind her of her own beauty.

Be Responsible

Understand that the key to happiness and self-improvement is in your hands and changes can only happen when you decide that you are ready to make them. If you are consistently unhappy, or need to change for improved health, then take control of your own situation and make the changes you need to make.

If you are healthy the way you are, then work on changing your attitude toward yourself so you can be happy. Most of the time negative feelings come from your past history or from people who make harsh judgments. If past experiences or beliefs are holding you back, find a way to get rid of those beliefs and make new choices about how you feel about yourself. If other people are projecting their negativity on you, ditch those people and make new friends.

Be Social

The way I have chosen to deal with my weight and my size has earned me love, admiration, and a very active social life, and that is what I hope for you, because you deserve it. You are no different from any size 2, size 4, size 6. . . . The size of clothing you wear may be a few numbers higher, but you deserve the same wonderful experiences every woman of every size and shape deserves.

Having an accepting, supportive, loving relationship with your body is vital for happiness. So when you're having one of those off days, turn to things that will inspire you to continue pursuing your new *Size Sexy* life.

let me tell you!

You become what you think, so think positively about yourself.

Validate Your *Size Sexy* Self

When you're having one of those off days, you can always turn to things that will inspire you to continue pursuing your new *Size Sexy* life. Movies and television shows are often a great source of inspiration, especially when they show us *Size Sexy* women living our lives to the fullest. If your confidence is flagging, take some time out to relax and watch successful, good-looking, happy, and self-confident *Size Sexy* women.

A few of my recommendations for *reel inspiration*, both on the big screen and on television include the following.

Babycakes

A full-figured and fabulous Ricki Lake stars as Grace Johnson, who works as a cosmetician in a funeral parlor. The *Size Sexy* Grace falls in love with pencil-thin ice skater Rob Harrison (Craig Sheffer), then launches a meticulous campaign to seduce her dream lover—and wins!

Hairspray

Both versions, the original 1988 Divine and Ricki Lake gem and the 2007 remake with the equally fabulous Nikki Blonsky, are great fun. The way these *Size Sexy* teens model enviable self-esteem is inspiring.

Muriel's Wedding

Toni Collette plays a *Size Sexy* woman who chases her dreams in this feel-great dramedy. Once she ventures out into the world and becomes an adventuress, a very sexy, athletic man falls in love with her, but she is the one who has to make the choice to stay with him or not.

Bridget Jones's Diary

Not everyone considers Renée Zellweger full-figured in this movie version of the best-selling book, but it is a fun story about a woman with definite body issues who doesn't ultimately let it stop her from living her life with gusto (and getting busy with two sexy men along the way!).

About Schmidt

The scene with Kathy Bates acting sexy while nude in the hot tub is sensational. Can you imagine what tremendous strength it took for a full-figured woman—or any other sized woman for that matter—to do that? Kathy Bates has been a wonderful role model in her real life, too. I always feel very inspired by the way she is able to exhibit her tremendous talent and be a full-figured, self-secure *Size Sexy* woman.

stella's secrets

Many of the great opera singers throughout history, regardless of their vocal ability, were big women with big breasts and beautiful décolletage. Supposedly their voices resonate throughout their entire body, and big rib cages and extra fat create depth of sound. Opera was and is the last frontier where there is no judgment on size; in fact, the bigger the better. *Size Sexy* to those in the opera world means gracefulness, talent, and a big voice—the bigger the better.

Bagdad Café

In this one, Marianne Sägebrecht stars as Jasmine, a German tourist whose husband leaves her stranded in the middle of the Nevada desert. After walking miles, toting her suitcase, Jasmine comes upon the Bagdad Café, a rundown truck stop and motel. Once there, she becomes a magical figure who brightens the lives of everyone around her. A beautifully *Size Sexy* actress, Marianne Sägebrecht shined in the movie, both as a sex symbol and a woman of strength.

More to Love

Full-figured Maryanne, played by Louise Werner, lives an isolated life as a secretary, where she experiences size discrimination from her coworkers, until she meets Fran, who helps her become a confident woman. This is a great movie for big girls and their admirers, to see women of all shapes and sizes portrayed as sexy, smart, savvy, and self-confident. It is also fascinating to watch the transformation—as Maryanne's self-esteem and life improves dramatically, her coworkers lives' fall apart.

Real Women Have Curves

The main character in this film is a full-figured Mexican-American teenager, played by the beautiful and talented America Ferrera. The movie reflects a mother-daughter relationship in which the mother sometimes doesn't handle her daughter's size well, but the heroine learns how to deal with those issues and proceeds to follow her dreams.

The Facts of Life

Way back in the 1980s, Mindy Cohn played the full-figured Natalie, a teenager who was funny, smart, and outgoing. For many, she was their favorite character because she was so endearing.

French and Saunders

French and Saunders features the fabulous, sassy, smart, and successful British comedian Dawn French. This hilarious show deals with a lot of the issues surrounding being a big woman and the positive sides of it. Dawn French herself is a full-figured woman who is intelligent and hilarious, and does a comedy standup routine in which she talks about big, beautiful women.

Less Than Perfect

The full-figured and beautiful Sara Rue plays Claude, a *Size Sexy* girl who works in a news network office, who becomes the personal assistant to the best anchorman. It also costars the funny, witty, beautiful *Size Sexy* Sherri Shepherd as Claude's friend Ramona. And I loved it because it had two big and beautiful women in the cast.

Living Single

This show, about four single American women who share a house together, had the talented and beautiful *Size Sexy* Queen Latifah as an assertive Khadijah and the *Size Sexy* Kim Coles as her sweet friend Synclaire. They were sensational role models for all full-figured women—real and reel winners.

Roseanne

The very full-figured Roseanne Barr portrayed a funny, confident, smart, and definitely sharp-tongued woman who ran the show—figuratively and literally, which I loved. She and costar John Goodman proved to the world that *Size Sexy* women—and men—have the same sexual urges and active sex lives as skinny people.

The Parkers

Not one, not two, but three lovely full-figured women in one cast! The lovely Mo'Nique as Nikki Parker; the *Size Sexy* Countess Vaughn as her daughter, Kim; and the funny, full-figured Yvette Wilson as Nikki's friend, Andell. All three are very funny, and according to Black Entertainment Television, *The Parkers* is the second-highest rated show among African-American households.

The Practice

The lovely and talented *Size Sexy* Camryn Manheim was so sensational in the role of a very passionate, eccentric, and powerful lawyer that she won an Emmy for her performance—winning one for all the *Size Sexy* beautiful women of the world.

*fabulous*quotes

"There are as many kinds of beauty as there are habitual ways of seeking happiness."
—Charles Baudelaire

Celebrate Your *Size Sexy* Self and Your New Self-Confidence

As you make gains in your self-esteem, take time to celebrate your victories. Reward your *Size Sexy* self by doing something that makes *you* feel good, something that supports the woman you already are or are now becoming. Don't wait to celebrate, go ahead and do it now—and do it often. Following are a few ideas to get you started.

- Throw a party, a fabulous, luscious party. Don't wait for a special occasion like a birthday or a holiday—the best reason for a celebration is the new you. It's good to flaunt your assets and to let your friends and loved ones help celebrate the new you!
- Do something you never dared to do before—try a sport, go skydiving, sign up for a painting class, or buy a pair of uncharacteristically sexy high heels.
- Luxuriate in a nice long bubble bath while listening to your favorite music. While soaking, plot the next step in your quest to more fully enjoy your life.
- Take a trip. Even if your destination is a two-hour drive away, take the time to seek adventure.
- Buy yourself a luxury item. It can be as small as a $35 pair of earrings or as expensive as you can realistically afford—just reward yourself with something that pleases you.
- Call a friend and invite him or her to a night out. Plan something that requires you to dress up and take your sexy self out into the world.
- Buy champagne and pop it open, even if you're the only one drinking.

Lighten Up

I especially hope this book has helped you lighten up on yourself and inspired you to make the necessary or desired changes in your lives, even if it's in little ways like changing the ways you think about yourself, your body, your self-image, and lifestyle, and improving upon and distancing yourself from the things that make you unhappy. I hope you will make it a goal to project yourselves to the world as a feminine, desirable, sexy, confident, fun, and sassy person and that you'll come to accept that your size may fluctuate, but your personality should not. Commit to always being a positive person, something that will color your reality in terms of your body, your shape, and your looks.

Give yourself the time to let everything you read in *Size Sexy* sink in, and use everything I have talked about in this book to help you create the new you—the happy, self-confident, self-accepting *Size Sexy* woman of style.

Check Your Readiness

And now it's time for your final *Size Sexy* test! But don't worry! This is a fun quiz, a quiz that will allow you to answer the all-important question: Are You Ready to Unleash Your Inner *Size Sexy* Self?

1. Were you inspired by my experiences as a *Size Sexy* woman?
2. Did you know that beautiful, full-figured, voluptuous women have been admired throughout history?
3. Now that you've read *Size Sexy*, are you excited to get it going on in your own life?
4. Do you realize that there is more to life than just your size?
5. Do you understand that being voluptuous is beautiful?
6. Do you understand that not having a model's body does not put you in the minority? The opposite is, in fact, true.
7. Do you believe that a full-figured woman can be *Size Sexy*?
8. Are you ready to celebrate your curves?
9. Do you understand that men love *Size Sexy* women? There's more to us, and of us, to love!
10. Are you ready to walk into a room with a positive, sexy attitude?
11. Are you ready to embrace positive thinking, self-confidence, and fabulousness?
12. Are you ready to flaunt your assets?
13. Are you ready to define your new personal style?
14. Are you ready to rule your world as a new *Size Sexy* "It" Girl?

Answers

We don't even need to tally your answers—of course, you're ready. And I know you are well on your way to becoming a happy, confident *Size Sexy* woman who lives her life to the fullest—with style, grace, romance, and *joie de vivre.*

I'd like to leave you fellow *Size Sexy* ladies with my favorite saying . . . *vive la glamour*!

appendix

stella's shopping guide

Designers Who Include Fabulous Clothing for *Size Sexy* Women in Their Collections

- Ellen Tracy
- Calvin Klein
- Anne Klein
- DKNY
- Juicy Couture
- Seven Jeans
- Baby Phat
- Liz Claiborne
- Eileen Fisher
- Marina Rinaldi
- Tadashi
- Lafayette 148
- Dana Buchman
- Jones New York
- Michael Kors
- Ralph Lauren
- Ed Hardy
- Tahari
- Vera Wang wedding gowns

Department Stores That Carry *Size Sexy* Sizes

- Macy's
- Bloomingdale's
- Saks Fifth Avenue
- Lord & Taylor
- Dillards
- Nordstrom

Size Sexy Specialty Stores

- Lane Bryant
- Avenue
- Ashley Stewart

Websites That Feature *Size Sexy* Fashions

www.beautypluspower.com
This shopping portal is reportedly the largest online directory of full-figured clothing options for women who wear a size 12 and above. It has a wide range of clothing options available, including costumes, formal and bridal, maternity, goth and punk, vintage and retro.

www.beyondtherack.com
Designer clothing at sale prices. Sales last two days, so you have to be quick. Sign up for e-mail announcements and you may claim designer duds at fabulous prices 65 percent and more below retail.

www.fashionfitsme.com
This a very cool shopping portal featuring plus-size clothes, including accessories and shoes, from a wide variety of department stores, online exclusive brands, and well-known designers.

http://fashionistaplus.blogspot.com
A fun blog to read, with fabulous fashion tips, and call-out buys for *Size Sexy* women.

www.hipsandcurves.com
A great site for finding sexy lingerie, including bras, panties, corsets, and hosiery. You'll even find fun costumes for sexy nights at home. They even have tips for men to help them figure out what size their *Size Sexy* lady wears.

www.missphit.com
Missphit was created by husband-and-wife team Yul and Christina Kwon who spent twenty years providing traditional women's plus-size clothing to local stores. Missphit's styles come from Christina and a talented team of designers who constantly search the world for ideas and inspiration. Christina studied fashion design at Esmod in Paris and has worked for designers Christian Dior and John Galliano.

www.onestopplus.com
They call themselves an "online mall for plus sizes." They feature brands like Woman Within, Roaman's, Jessica London, Avenue, Chadwick's Woman, Tallissime, Ellos, Comfort Choice, KingSize, and BrylaneHome.

www.pasazz.net
This shopping directory provides long lists of shopping websites, organized by the type of clothing desired: casual, formal, swim, bridal, teen, lingerie, etc. They also have wide-width shoes and accessory sites listed.

Size Sexy Clothing Stores with Websites

Minx Fashion Shoppe
322 Main Street #1
Seal Beach, CA 90740
562-496-3500
www.minxshoppe.com

Curvaceous Chic Woman
P.O. Box 37185
Richmond, VA 23234
804-425-7329
www.curvaceouschicwoman.com

Canadian Stores

Voluptuous
4 locations in Ontario:
Dufferin Mall, Vaughan Mills,
Square One Mall, Scarbrough Town Centre
Head office: 416-533-3298
www.voluptuousclothing.com

CurveConscious.com
Totem Mall
Fort St. John, BC V1J6C7
1-877-A-Curvy-U
www.curveconscious.com

United Kingdom

Sosienna
The Hollies, Fenwick
Doncaster South Yorkshire
Great Britain, DN60HA
0844-800-6967
www.sosienna.com

New Zealand

Bella Chic
38 Turnberry Drive
Wattle Cove, Auckland
New Zealand
www.bellachic.co.nz

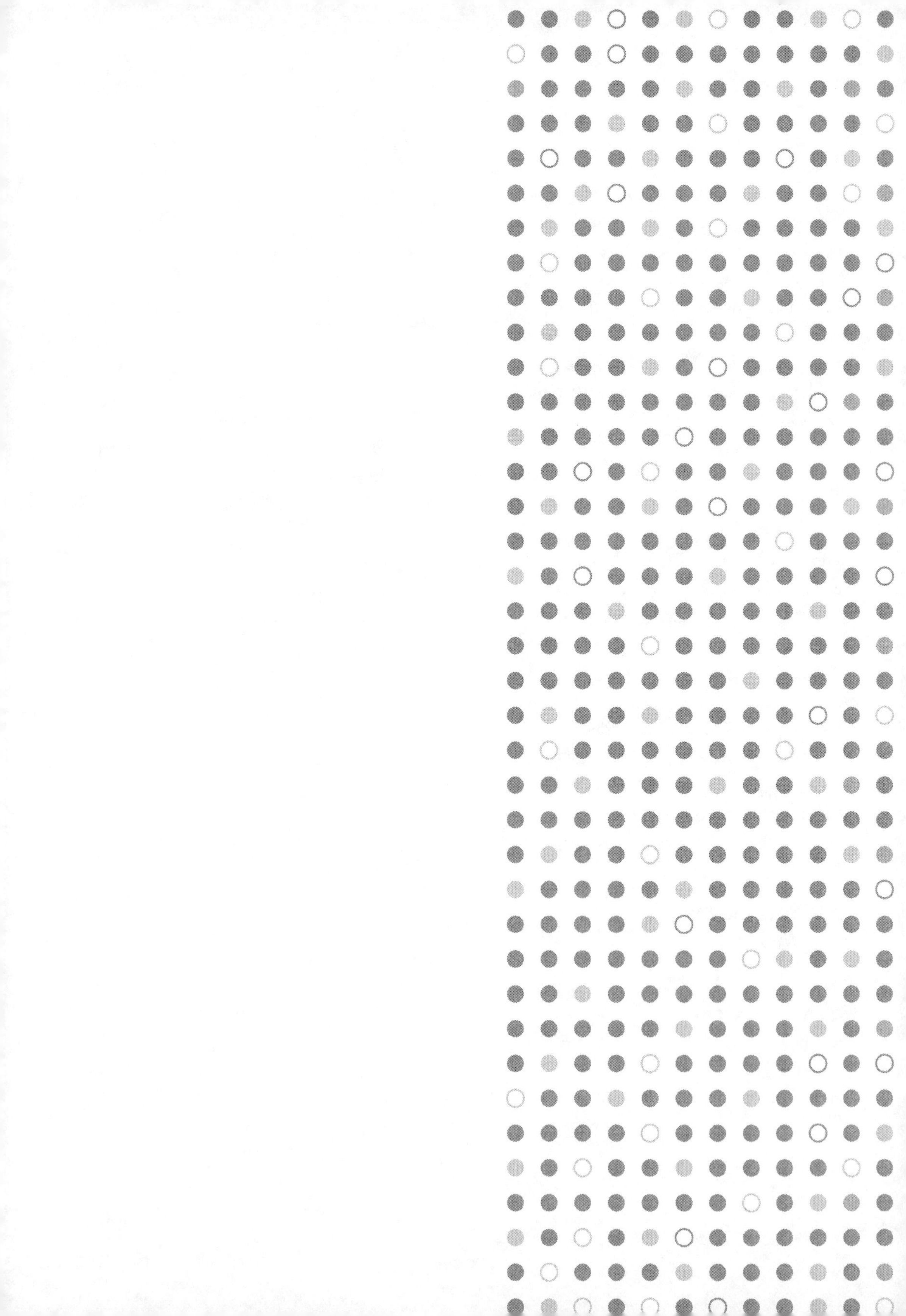

index

about the author

STELLA ELLIS was born in Israel, speaks eight languages, has lived, studied, and worked abroad and in the United States—and has resided here for over twenty years. She has worked in the fashion industry, TV, and modeling. Stella appeared in Madonna's book *Sex*, and was also Thierry Mugler's model and Jean Paul Gaultier's full-figured muse. Visit her at *www.stellaellis.net.*